Hema Malini

A writer-journalist and film-critic, **Bhawana Somaaya** is the recipient of the Mahila Shiromani Award (1990) for her contribution to the field of journalism and her various prominent titles published over the years. She has regularly contributed to various columns in *Sunday Observer, Afternoon, Janmabhoomi Pravasi, Hindustan Times, The Hindu, The Pioneer* and the *Newstime.* She is also the author of well-known titles like *Amitabh Bachchan – The Legend, Salaam Bollywood, Take-25, The Story So Far* and *Cinema: Images & Issues.*

OTHER LOTUS TITLES:

Aitzaz Ahsan	*The Indus Saga: The Making of Pakistan*
Alam Srinivas	*Storms in the Sea Wind: Ambani vs Ambani*
Amir Mir	*The True Face of Jehadis: Inside Pakistan's Terror Networks*
Chaman Nahal	*Silent Life: Memoirs of a Writer*
Duff Hart-Davis	*Honorary Tiger: The Life of Billy Arjan Singh*
Frank Simoes	*Frank Unedited*
Frank Simoes	*Frank Simoes' Goa*
M.G. Devasatayam	*JP in Jail: An Uncensored Account*
M.J. Akbar	*India: The Siege Within*
M.J. Akbar	*Kashmir: Behind the Vale*
M.J. Akbar	*Nehru: The Making of India*
M.J. Akbar	*Riot after Riot*
M.J. Akbar	*The Shade of Swords*
M.J. Akbar	*Byline*
M.J. Akbar	*Blood Brothers: A Family Saga*
Meghnad Desai	*Nehru's Hero Dilip Kumar: In the Life of India*
Nayantara Sahgal (ed.)	*Before Freedom: Nehru's Letters to His Sister*
Neesha Mirchandani	*Wisdom Song: The Life of Baba Amte*
Rohan Gunaratna	*Inside Al Qaeda*
Maj. Gen. Ian Cardozo	*Param Vir: Our Heroes in Battle*
Maj. Gen. Ian Cardozo	*The Sinking of Khukri*
Maj. R.P. Singh, Kanwar Rajpal Singh	*Sawai Man Singh II of Jaipur: Life and Legend*
Mushirul Hasan	*India Partitioned. 2 Vols*
Mushirul Hasan	*John Company to the Republic*
Mushirul Hasan	*Knowledge, Power and Politics*
Rachel Dwyer	*Yash Chopra: Fifty Years of Indian Cinema*
Satish Jacob	*From Hotel Palestine Baghdad*
Shrabani Basu	*Spy Princess: The Life of Noor Inayat Khan*
V. Srinivasan	*New Age Management Philosophy from Ancient Indian Wisdom*
Veena Sharma	*Kailash Mansarovar: A Sacred Journey*
Verghese Kurien, as told to Gouri Salvi	*I Too Had a Dream*

FORTHCOMING TITLES:

Ajit Bhattacharjea	*Sheikh Abdullah: A Biography*
A. Salam Qureishi	*An Indian in Silicon Valley*

Hema Malini

THE AUTHORIZED BIOGRAPHY

BHAWANA SOMAAYA

WITH A FOREWORD BY
GULZAR

LOTUS COLLECTION
ROLI BOOKS

Lotus Collection

First published in hardback 2007
Paperback edition 2008
The Lotus Collection
An imprint of
Roli Books Pvt. Ltd.
M-75, G.K. II Market, New Delhi 110 048 .
Phones: ++91 (011) 2921 2271, 2921 2782
2921 0886, Fax: ++91 (011) 2921 7185
E-mail: roli@vsnl.com
Website: rolibooks.com
Also at
Varanasi, Bangalore, Jaipur, Kolkata & Mumbai

Cover design: Aarti Subramanium
Layout design: Narendra Shahi
Production: Kumar Raman
Photographs on pgs. viii, xx courtesy: Dabboo Ratnani
Pg. 192 courtesy: Gautam Rajadhyaksha
Cover photograph courtesy: Subi Samuel

Price: Rs
ISBN: 978-81-7436-650-4

Typeset in Minion by Roli Books Pvt. Ltd. and
printed at Rakmo Press, Okhla, New Delhi - 110 020

For my two sisters,
Jiji Pravina Thakkar and
Sarla Rajani who have been
an integral part of my growing up

Contents

Acknowledgements

Madhuri Poojary for her undiminished patience and perseverance in typing out several drafts of this manuscript.

Deepa Karmalkar for checking the connections and making valid corrections.

Catherine Lewis for aiding in co-ordination, and Hema's cousin Prabha Raghavan for sorting out Hema's file pictures.

Foreword

It is my privilege to be associated with a book that involves two of my favourite people, actress and dancer Hema Malini, and journalist and friend, Bhawana Somaaya.

Hema and I have travelled many scripts together through many decades. As a filmmaker who directed her in four films, I would say that she is as good or as bad as the script or the director.

A lot has been written about her beauty and stardom but what has always appealed to me about her as a filmmaker is her regality. There is a halo about her presence and while for most artistes, this aura extends from their creativity to their personality, in her case, the dignity is transmitted from real to reel. Take any of her old or new films, she may play a rustic tangewali as in *Sholay* or a dacoit in *Ramkali* but she leaves her unmistakable stamp.

It is a misconception that Hema is shy and withdrawn. My first impression of her when I met her on the sets of *Andaaz* was of a spirited, self-reliant person. I had written the dialogues of the film and director Ramesh Sippy wanted me to explain the voice to her.

While working with her on her scenes, I discovered that she has a sharp mind in learning dialogues and is very clear about her goals. As early as 1971 she told me that no matter how busy she got with films, she would never quit dancing. 'I will make sure that I hold at least two performances a year,' she said.

Today, I marvel at her clarity of thought and her vision. It calls for extraordinary discipline and determination to remain as focussed as she has been. She has mentioned in the book somewhere that dance for her is bhakti ... This is evident in her commitment and her endeavour to constantly expand her horizons. It is very rare for film personalities to pursue other interests outside cinema because show business is a very demanding profession. But despite a flourishing career as an actress, marriage and kids, Hema has continued with her passion for dance.

There are no doubts that in the history of Hindi cinema Hema Malini has had the longest reign as a number one star. No heroine before or after her has enjoyed her position or power and it's to her credit that she has never misused her superstardom. On the contrary, despite several limitations and hurdles she has pushed herself to the optimum level to explore varied mediums like television, direction and at the moment Parliament.

The media projects her as a traditional woman but her choices in life prove that she is more liberal than most of the slogan-shouting feminists we know about. Her unconventional marriage could not have occurred without her conviction to walk the path untrodden. And the fact that she has been able to sustain this deviant relationship tells a lot about her courage and endurance.

There is a side to Hema's personality that is very gregarious and affectionate which she takes great care to not reveal to outsiders. I have seen glimpses of her effervescence at my shootings. Her closest companion those days was her aunt (her mother's youngest sister) popularly addressed as Shanta aunty by Hema's colleagues. I called her Captain aunty because she always wore the sun cap at outdoor stints. Through *Khushboo*, *Kinara* and later *Meera* I have been privy to many bonding moments between the two women. There was always a lot of banter on the

Gulzar directing Hema Malini in Kinara.

sets when they were together ... She was the only one I think with whom Hema had her defences completely down.

What is intriguing about Hema is that her reserves build up just as suddenly. Strangers were always uncomfortable about being in her presence and she did not make any effort to put them at ease. She once confessed to me that she tried not to be so restrained but when in public, her body language altered by reflex action. I remember her expression when she said so. At that moment she had looked and felt completely helpless.

My heroine Shabana Azmi on the sets of *Namkeen* introduced

author Bhawana Somaaya to me way back in 1980. I liked her instantly, particularly her surname Somaaya. It has such a beautiful sound to it that I intend using it as the name of one of my characters in a film some day.

Over the years Somaaya has penned several insightful features on me, followed my career diligently with constructive criticism. On my part I'm familiar with her columns and books and always recognized her writings without having to read the byline below. I have been an admirer of her objective analysis of films and her fearless stand on ideological issues.

Somaaya lends her keen observations as a journalist to this book. She projects the anxieties and the loneliness of the superstar and the woman with rare compassion and restraint. There are several revealing moments in the book when the reader can sense the actor's desolation but there is no attempt on the part of the writer to sensationalize those moments.

On the contrary, the author documents the anecdotes like a quiet observer wading through the intricate web of fantasy and fiction. She lets the reel overlap the real and vice versa, to an extent that many a times it is difficult to determine who is the alter ego between the subject and her voiceover.

The biography traces various phases in Hema Malini's life. There is the fragrance of vintage decades, many moods, and changing patterns. Some of them leave a haunting impression – the early days, describing mother Jaya Chakravarti's trip to Amangudi ... and later when Hema tries to fit into the jungle world of films. Her attraction to Dharmendra, her attachment to her guruma and her recurring obsession with Lord Krishna are interesting revelations attractively strung together. Some of the chapters particularly have a brilliant summing up.

Somaaya has done as wonderful a job in putting Hema Malini's life into words as Jaya Chakravarti did for her daughter in real life. My congratulations to both.

Mumbai, July 2006 GULZAR

Preface

To agree to a biography reflects a state of mind. It means you are ready to reflect on your past actions. Part of me was ready for the exercise for I believed that not analysing meant escaping. Unless I'm able to accept myself with all my inadequacies, how can I, in all sincerity, complete my relationships with my dear ones? My daughters insisted that I should. At least this way they could connect with all that happened to me when they were not a part of my life.

I bided my time, asked myself if I was willing to share my private world with strangers ... I felt hesitant. Connecting with your fans via your films is one thing and exposing your heartbreaks and the struggle that made the dream possible quite another. Time went by ... Then one evening, as I was driving to my new home in Goregaon, I saw the crimson sun dive into the sea. The moment was a reminder that the best of things have to end sometime. Something resolved for me that moment ... I had made up my mind ...

My mother always said that we assume that we make decisions. But it is destiny all the time that holds our finger and leads us to our karma ... I would not have been able to achieve all I did in my life and career without the passion and devotion of one woman, my mother. She has been the signal of all my turning points, both on celluloid as well as on stage. Before I plunged into the final decision of unveiling the varied phases of my life via this book, I needed to seek her approval. As always, she surprised me with her candour. 'You should have done it a long time ago ... And you need not be scared of people's reactions because you can do it your way, the way you always have.'

I guess that's what I've done, spoken from the heart. This one is for you Amma ...

Mumbai, July 2006 HEMA MALINI

Prologue

In the late 1970s when I began my career as a film journalist, Hema Malini was the reigning queen of Hindi films. Coined as the Dream Girl, moviegoers missed a heartbeat every time Hema flashed her radiant smile into the camera. Her dancing eyes and characteristic voice lit up the screen every time she appeared in the frame. For her fans, she was the ideal woman to take home to mama.

Off screen, Hema struck a formidable presence at film studios and public functions. Always surrounded by an entourage, Hema wore a stern expression and seldom smiled at anybody. As a rule, she was unapproachable to everyone and that included filmmakers and journalists.

And yet strangely, both could not do without her. The former, because Hema was the most saleable star of the film firmament, and the latter because she was the most controversial star of the decade.

As a budding journalist getting newly acquainted with show business, Hema Malini was an intimidating experience. I have vivid memories of my first encounter with the actress. Assigned to cover a shooting of her new film *Hum Tere Aashiq Hain* in an Andheri studio, I was instructed to get a quote from the actress for our cover story that month. Only a few months old on the job, I was terrified of returning to the office without the task completed. I somehow managed to grab Hema's attention as she was walking out of the set. Standing beside her car, she heard my question in silence and in response gave me a freezing look that left me paralysed.

Much later she confided to my editor that she did not co-operate with me because I had attempted talking to her while she was walking and she considered that bad manners.

I made sure I stayed out of Hema Malini's orbit after that. But work commitments compelled me to cross her territory from time to time and the brief interludes, for some mysterious reasons, always provoked hostile reactions.

To give a few examples: On the sets of Gulzar's unreleased *Devdas,* Hema was annoyed because I was staring at her while she was putting glycerine in her eyes … On the sets of *The Burning Train*, she was annoyed because I caught an unguarded tear trickle down her face … and on the sets of *Razia Sultan* because I had accompanied my colleague who was interviewing her and participated in the discussion.

It was only a decade later, while penning a biography booklet that formed a part of the '*g*' magazine I edited, that Hema and I made truce. In an extensive interview spanning her long career, she discussed her childhood, marriage and children with an alarming honesty.

We met again a few years later when Hema completed her debut film as a director, *Dil Aashna Hai*. She appeared exhausted but excited with the attention she was receiving. 'I am thrilled to have made my first film but I hope this is not going to deter other directors from offering me future acting assignments,' she said innocently.

At every turning point Hema was evolving, becoming more aware and wholesome. In the winter of 2000 when she released my book *Take 25* at the Kerala Film Festival in Thiruvanantha-puram, she mentioned reading the above references in my earlier book *Salaam Bollywood* and together we had a great laugh over the time gone by. It was a warm afternoon in the scenic atmosphere of Kerala and we bonded both as women and as professionals.

A year later, when she was preparing for her new dance ballet *Draupadi*, she had invited me for the premiere recital and I had written a thought-provoking column on the complexities of her portrayal in my paper. One early morning she telephoned me to compliment on the story and also to suggest if I would consider writing a book chronicling her sojourn as a dancer. 'Today everyone remembers me only as a film star but there would be no Hema Malini without her dance ... I have been dancing since the age of six and clearly remember every moment when I learnt a new *adavu* (dance step). Dance is my oldest and most loyal companion. I don't want all my memories to scatter away without telling the world about my sacrifices. As artistes we owe it to our fans. Unless we share our hardships how will they be inspired to face up to similar challenges in their lives?'

This book is about the actress who bloomed and transformed with the various roles she performed on screen. Some accused that she survived her long career on her sheer beauty. Others attributed her success to her scintillating screen presence, but all of them agreed that she was extremely focussed, disciplined and enormously lucky.

It is about the artiste for whom dance is not just a passion but a way of life. Through the art form she transports from the material to the sublime world. Most importantly, the book tells about the woman Hema Malini. It is a result of our innumerable conversations held at her home over the months. In different settings and different moods, the memories of those moments come gushing … Her ringing laughter over the dinning table as she elaborated on Dharmendra's food preferences. 'At his farmhouse in Lonavala they serve hot parathas with lassi and all of them drink ghee directly from a katori … '

The sunny afternoon when we sat on the swing, in her verandah discussing mundane domestic issues, Hema was in a philosophic mood and talked about *karma*, all the time staring at a crow-lined skyline … I remember the desolate evening when we met up for dinner and chatted till late night in her room upstairs … She was in a confiding mood and spoke about the cross of stardom and how it affects the numero uno actor. The frequent afternoons spent in her living room with mother Jaya Chakravarti sitting amidst us in her favourite chair, her two pet dogs lying at her feet and the phone ringing non-stop … Hema would heave a deep sigh and say, 'This is a mad house … '

With her classic Indian features and fairly traditional grooming, one associates her with a certain conservative quality. It is only when you interact with her that you discover that she is not only progressive but also has a good sense of humour. There is a natural grace to her that makes her travel through fragile, complex experiences with restraint and poise. Her life is about someone who transformed every obstacle into an opportunity.

There are so many hues and numerous moods. On one level she is the simple South Indian girl content with eating curd rice, surrounded by her children and family. On the other, she is the evolved Krishna devotee immersed in the *madhurya bhav* for her Lord. I'm not sure if the book captures all these colours. It's not easy for any writer to perceive her subject the way she perceives herself. One tries but eventually the writer projects her own observations. This book is no exception. They are my observations of Hema Malini. Her life in flashbacks and flash-forwards, for memories cannot be on call.

BHAWANA SOMAAYA

Shlokas and the Sound of Tatu Kazhi

It was a cloudy August morning many summers ago when V.S.R. Chakravarti, employed with the Medical Council of India, came to see his wife Jaya off at the Delhi railway station. He had not expected to feel as gloomy as he did.

Jaya Chakravarti was seven months pregnant and leaving for her parents' home in Tamil Nadu for her delivery, accompanied by her two sons, Kannan (four) and Jagannath (two).

Even as Chakravarti pierced through the crowded platform to find place for his family and settle the luggage, he caught his wife's expression.

Jaya looked desolate. She had been dreading this moment of parting from her husband and had delayed it for as long as she could. But now, she had to embark on the journey. Tears welled up in her eyes, but Jaya held back. Chakravarti admired her restraint. She had always been a very strong woman and that was part of her attraction.

Facing Page: *From a tender age Hema became addicted to the beat of tatu kazhi. Dance became a part of her identity, her companion.*

As the train blew the final whistle, Chakravarti descended from the bogie and stood by the window, looking at his wife. Dressed in a sky-blue sari, her long, lustrous hair tied in a braid and vermilion shining between her kohl-lined sparkling eyes, Jaya looked dazzling. As the train began chugging off the platform, Chakravarti felt a pang. He realized that he would not see his wife for another four months.

Sitting by the train window, Jaya thought of Amangudi, her hometown in Trichinapalli. Their house stood beside an ancient temple festooned with trees. It was a Vaishnav family tradition to wake up to the clanging of temple bells every morning. Jaya's father, Parasarathy Iyengar, was a religious man and the children had been brought up to participate in the temple aarti. The pundit recited the *Gayatri shloka* and they repeated after him. Jaya loved the sound of the chanting, particularly the *Lakshmi sutram* describing the various incarnations of goddess Lakshmi.

Special prayers were reserved for special festivals. Dassera was Jaya's favourite festival and after almost five years, she was returning home in time for the auspicious celebrations.

Down south, it is a tradition that families begin preparing weeks in advance for the *golu* (navratri) festival. Curtains and carpets are laundered, rooms painted and doors dressed up with jasmine flowers. It is a custom during these auspicious days to reserve a room for worshipping the deities. A special set comprising nine steps, signifying the nine days of the festival is designed. Wrapped in white fabric, each step signifies a different theme and is decorated accordingly.

Every evening, for nine consecutive days, the entire house is lit up with earthern lamps. Little children from neighbouring homes are invited to perform cultural activities to entertain the gods and are rewarded with gifts. To ensure that there are no hindrances during the festival, the lady of the house allots specific responsibilities to each member of the family. This year Jaya was assigned the creative task of decorating the walls of the puja room, and she impressed everyone by painting portraits of the divine goddesses.

Bereft of adequate company, she spent most of her time engrossed in violin lessons and painting portraits on the walls. She enjoyed it immensely. Women painters were not as common then as they are today, and visitors to the house were full of admiration for her vibrant images of the goddesses – Lakshmi, Durga and Saraswati.

Goddess Lakshmi standing on a lotus, adorning a necklace was Jaya's favourite. A coincidence but a few days later, on 15 October midnight, on Dassera day, Jaya delivered her third child, a divinely beautiful daughter. She named her Hema Malini. The word means divine and is derived from a *Lakshmi sutram.* 'My mother told me later that she painted the goddesses because she saw them recurrently in her dreams … ' says Hema Malini.

As a child, Hema was all the time in the company of her older brothers and being the youngest, they bullied her. 'I followed them everywhere but was unable to cope with their rough and tough games. My mother disapproved of me playing in the sun with them. She'd pull me inside the house and plaster my hair with oil. Many hours later, freshly bathed and rested, I would wait for them to return and tell me stories about their adventures.'

As she grew older, Hema discovered that her mother nursed special dreams for her future. They were perhaps remains of Jaya's own dormant desires sacrificed at the altar of marriage, which she now hoped to realize through her daughter. Jaya grew up in a family where music was all around her and it is not surprising that she was attracted to all things artistic. She was a voracious reader and a prolific writer who contributed regular columns in Tamil magazines. She was well versed in classical art and could also play the violin effortlessly. However, she nursed no ambition or desire to pursue these as a career. For her daughter, however, Jaya was determined to groom her as a dancer – that was her dream and her goal.

Chakravarti briefly served in the Ministry of Labour and Employment. Later, he joined the Employees' State Insurance Corporation (ESIC) in Delhi and enjoyed an illustrious career

The most talked about child artiste in the capital. Little Hema in one of her early performances.

While he vigilantly watched over their two sons, Kannan and Jagannath, he entrusted his daughter to the care of his efficient wife. Jaya followed her instinct and enrolled her little girl for formal training in Bharatanatyam under the tutelage of Guru Tara Ramaswamy. The first time Hema was demonstrated the *adavus*, her knees hurt terribly. But she was not allowed to bunk lessons. 'You will get used to it,' her mother explained gently and she was right. Within a few weeks, Hema was dancing without complaints, and before the end of the year, even performing at public gatherings.

Based in Delhi, opportunities to perform before ministers came frequently. These included the then President Rajendra Prasad and other prominent dignitaries like Queen Elizabeth. There weren't too many young performers in those days, and as a result Hema was amongst the most talked about child artiste in the capital. 'I loved the attention and adulation, and for the time being forgot the aching knees,' recalls Hema Malini today.

'Over the years the recitals became a part of my life. Before going on stage, Amma had a guru mantra for me that always worked miracles. "Concentrate, don't get nervous, don't make mistakes," she'd urge. She would make me bow before the idol of Nataraja and say a silent prayer. Something would happen in the pit of my stomach just before the curtain rose. Then, when the music started and the lights came on, I would feel in total control again. The confidence emerged from the fact that Amma was guarding me from the wings, and her sheer presence reassured me that nothing could go wrong.'

In Delhi, the Chakravartis lived in the official government house in a colony near Gole Market. Outside the cottage was a well-mowed lawn and a verandah with pillars where the family sat together every evening. A long corridor separated the kitchen from the rooms. 'Amma spent a lot of time cooking in the kitchen. We always ate together, our plates laid on a slightly raised wooden plank. Sometimes when Appa got late at work, Amma would wait for him but she would sit across us and serve generous replenishments on our plates,' states Hema.

'A part-time maid helped her with coconut grinding and cleaning. Appa always helped Amma with the kitchen chores. After dinner, while we children ran out to play, he would help her clear the dishes ... Strangely, I was never forced to learn housework or cooking and I did not miss them. Difficult chores like carrying mattresses and rolling them on the cot were Appa's duty, and later, my elder brother Kannan took charge,' she relates.

Even after all these years, whenever Hema is in Delhi, memories of her childhood come rushing back. 'When we were kids, every time we had to visit the railway station, Appa would hire two vehicles – a tonga to carry the luggage, and a Victoria for the rest of us. Appa would warn the two buggiwallas to ride close to each other so that he could keep an eye on the luggage. My brothers and I looked forward to these rides. The Victorias were so magnificent. The regality, however, vanished as soon as we reached the station. The Delhi Railway Station was always overcrowded and noisy. When the train arrived, everyone jostled with one another to get on to the bogie. In those days there was no such thing like reservation of seats. The passengers would climb on to the compartments and block space. We carried old sheets from home to spread across the seats so that nobody occupied them. I loved sitting by the window … The breeze playing on my face and songs playing in my head …

'I remember the cold Delhi winters and the woollens my appa would buy for us. This excited us so much that we would wear one sweater over the other. During the winter months it was so cold that everyone usually stayed indoors. However, I could not miss my dance classes. Dancing in winter is very deceptive. As long as you are on stage, you feel protected, but the moment you stepped out, the cold breeze would send shivers down your spine. At such times Appa would wrap me in a heavy overcoat, firmly clasped with a belt.'

Hema also has warm memories of Delhi summers when everyone would sleep on the terrace, under the open skies and the stars, 'My brothers and I had a great time playing hide and seek ... And when it rained, Appa would protectively hold an umbrella over my head while riding me to my class on his bicycle. The dance school was far away in the city and in those days the bicycle was our only mode of transport.'

On days when the bicycle was not in good condition, Chakravarti and his little princess travelled by the local transport. It was a long walk from the bus stop to their home, but Hema made sure to firmly clasp her father's hand. 'Appa believed that walking was the best exercise for the human body. He referred to it as his personal "Nataraj Transport Service". Everyone in the family walked regularly. I walked from my dance class to home. My brothers walked to school and Amma walked to the market to pick up her daily groceries. In those days, nobody hired transport for short distances. Some of them did travel by the rusty three-wheelers but we were never allowed to because Appa disapproved of their rough driving. Those long walks are still etched in my memory. … Appa and I hardly exchanged any words but in that silence, there was a deep bonding. He was never physically demonstrative of his love and affection, but his firm grip over my hand was very reassuring,' she reminisces fondly.

The family seldom had social outings but they never missed an opportunity to attend a dance concert. Once, Hindi cinema's reigning star Vyjayanthimala was performing Bharatanatyam at Delhi's Sapru House, and the Chakravartis had gone to watch her performance. Vyjayanthimala was electric on stage and even today, Hema remembers her rustling *kanjeevaram* sari, her sparkling black eyes and her long artistic fingers. 'She looked ethereal. After the show, she shook hands with me and spoke a few encouraging words. That was a magical moment for me and more so for my mother,' she adds.

The Chakravartis were full of admiration for Vyjayanthimala as a dancer. Hema remembers her parents often discussing her performances at home. 'Appa had a keen eye to observe and understand the skills required to organize such shows, but Amma was more interested in the art form.' For Jaya Chakravarti, every recital they attended was an opportunity to groom Hema into a better dancer. When they got home, she discussed the performance in detail – highlighting the strengths and the limitations of the dancer. Hema was always a silent participant in these discussions, internalizing her parents' opinions and unconsciously striving for higher accomplishments. Jaya Chakravarti had big dreams for her daughter and was prepared to pay the price, to sacrifice and surrender. For the realization of these dreams she worked tirelessly towards it. She would monitor Hema's walk, her posture. She tutored her how to walk with her shoulders pushed back and how to sit gracefully like a lady. At night while tucking her into bed, or dressing her up for school in the morning, Jaya would always revise her dance lessons. This became a habit with Hema, and soon, no matter where she went and what she did, Hema was always unknowingly practising her *adavus, mudras* and *abhinaya.*

A family photograph: *Hema with father V.S.R. Chakravarti and mother Jaya. Seen also are her brothers R. Kannan and R. Jagannath.*

Hema cannot recall a defining moment, but she gradually began to enjoy dance. She became addicted to the beat of the *tatu kazhi* on the floor, which she describes as almost hypnotic. Triveni Kala Sangam was a prominent dance academy in Delhi and it was considered a privilege to be tutored by Guru Ramaswami Pillai. Hema looked forward to these classes, but she did not want to dance all the time. Like other children, she wanted to play; to stand by the window and stare at the passers-by, to laze around and listen to the gossip of the old women; or simply tag along with her brothers. However, her rigorous routine allowed little scope for such indulgence.

She studied at the Madrasi Higher Secondary School along with her older siblings but had little interaction with her classmates. If she was not at school, then she was engrossed in her homework. Moreover, when she finished her lessons, she had to go for her dance class. Sometimes she missed having friends but because she was extremely shy, she did not know how to cultivate them. 'When I saw other children playing in the neighbourhood I wondered what they laughed about. I could not fathom their joys and I am sure they found me equally baffling. There were times when I wanted to be like them and play mischief, something that provoked my mother.'

On such occasions, Jaya employed a unique and constructive way of reprimanding her daughter. Every time Hema disobeyed her or made her angry, Jaya would punish Hema by making her practise three Bharatanatyam dance items – *Alaaripu, Jatiswaram* and *Shabdam*.

Hema was so well versed in these dances that even if she was just woken from sleep, she could perform them with her eyes closed. By then, slightly defiant, Hema insisted that she would dance only behind closed doors. Too exhausted to protest, Jaya would relent. 'Once inside my room, I would loudly sing the song and thump my feet on the floor faking the impression that I was dancing, when in fact I was only doing the footwork without the accompanying hand movements. It gave me a sense of power and achievement to cheat on my mother. Still young, the enormity of the precious art had not yet dawned on me. The realization was to come much later … ,' she recalls with a naughty twinkle in her doe-eyes.

Her major distraction in those days was her younger brother, Jagannath. The elder one Kannan, always sober, was protective of her. The pranks usually came from Jagan. 'He would, all the time contrive new tricks to exasperate me. Every time I began dancing, he would stand around and make faces. Naturally, I would burst into giggles and get fired by Amma for not concentrating. This was a daily routine. Jagan would irritate me only to make Amma yell at me. That was his moment of triumph and glory. He would run around me, victoriously clapping his hands, and I would burst into tears. Such childishness, but so important for growing up,' she says fondly.

The family had little interaction with anyone in the colony except the Bhattacharyas who lived some distance away. The Bhattacharyas also had a daughter almost the same age as Hema, and sometimes the two families got together for a meal at each other's homes. Those were joyous occasions when the four kids got together and created a riot. Often these moments got interrupted because Hema had other commitments. Jaya Chakravarti had enrolled her for an additional class in music, since she believed that a basic knowledge of *sur* and *taal* would evolve her into a more competent dancer. Jaya was keen that Hema pursue it as an academic degree, and to please her, Hema reluctantly appeared for the third and the fourth music exams, only to back out during the finals. 'My life was too hectic to overcrowd it with yet another art form. Amma was disappointed, but after a while she understood and stopped pressurizing. She accepted that it was better for me to prosper in one medium rather than scatter away in different directions.'

But music remained an integral part of Hema's growing-up years. 'We woke up every morning to the strains of Amma's violin and Appa's recitation of *shlokas* and unconsciously echoed the chantings while going through our routine motions. However, music never belonged to me, the way dance did ... Dance was my identity, the companion I never had. I am not sure if my mother felt as passionately about her music or may be she never expressed it because her circumstances were so different.'

Married at the tender age of thirteen, Jaya was weighed down by the responsibilities of marriage and motherhood. But Chakravarti was sensitive enough not to let his wife's passion for art forms wither away in routine chores. He made sure that she completed her matriculation, and in time to come, enrolled her to specialize in the Hindi language (Jaya was a 'Prabhakar' degree holder in the subject). When he discovered her flair for painting, he purchased an easel for her to pursue the talent at her leisure. Years later, when she was drawn to writing, Chakravarti encouraged her to pen thoughts on paper.

All through her growing years Hema remembers her mother using time productively, 'She had multiple interests and it always baffled me how she juggled her varied activities without it ever coming in the way of her domestic responsibilities. She used to sing, cook, supervise my dance lessons and even give private tuition in Hindi. We always had a lot of visitors dropping by at our home and interestingly, those who came to meet Appa were distinctly different from Amma's guests.'

Her father's guests were from the world of academics and would come attired formally. Some of them came dressed in dhotis too, their foreheads smeared with *naman* (Vaishnav symbol made on forehead). They were spiritual leaders who held discourses. The sessions were held thrice a year and usually extended over two days. A day prior to the discourse, colourful pandals were put up in the lawn outside. It was an indicator for the neighbouring kids to arrive and play in the open space. But entry to these discourses was only restricted to the South Indian community. Chakravarti who was well connected with the scholars in Madras was in charge of organizing these events. The sessions lasted for a couple of days and covered various subjects including the Bhagavad Gita, *Bhagwatam* and *Ramayan*. Trained cooks well versed in Iyengar customs were hired to prepare special food for the pundits.

When the session commenced the children gathered around in the front row. Enchanted by the proceedings they would huddle close to the loudspeakers. 'The scholars were great orators and even though we did not understand all that was communicated, we were mesmerized by the Sanskrit renditions followed by translations in Tamil and English. Only later, when we turned older, we discovered that they were patrons of Acharya Ramanuja and their teachings were based on his philosophy,' says Hema. 'As descendants of Vaishnavas, my faith in religion is natural. This explains my deep attachment to the ISKCON temple and Lord Krishna. The devotion is a result of the conditioning of so many years … I was in awe of my father's guests but greatly attracted to my mother's visitors too … '

Her mother's guests came from the world of music and art and were invariably appreciative of Hema's blossoming beauty and talent. 'I was never told so directly, but sometimes I would overhear Amma's friends complimenting me, then she would quickly change the topic because she did not want me to get swollen-headed with all the attention. In all these years, she has never overtly praised me. Even when I asked for approval, she was not willing to commit herself. All that she would say is, "you are okay," but it was always said with such conviction that it reassured me instantly.'

Being in Delhi presented Hema many opportunities to perform in front of various dignitaries. Apart from dance, Hema also participated in other carricular activities. Hema seen here with renowned cartoonist Shankar.

Costumes and Camera

Hema was putting on her anklets, getting ready for the evening class, when she saw her mother in conversation with her dance tutor outside her room. The two folded hands in the traditional *namaskar*, then went their separate ways. This was an indicator to the little girl that her mother had yet again, in pursuit of excellence, replaced her tutor. Tutors were replaced every six months. Unlike other dancers who go through a lifetime devoted to only one guru, Hema had the rare opportunity of learning from a number of teachers in her long, illustrious career.

In the very beginning Hema was put into a general class where she learnt dance along with many other students. 'Those were fun days and whenever any of us missed a step, we hid behind the other in order not to be noticed by the teacher,' says Hema.

A year later, Jaya shifted Hema to Smt Indira, a student of Kalakshetra who was very good, but an unusually strict teacher. 'She laid the perfect foundation of Bharatanatyam in Kalakshetra style for me. This was my first private tuition and there was no way I could escape her critical eye. Without a doubt I would have

Facing Page: *A star is born: Hema in a still from* Gora Aur Kala.

prospered continuing with her except that she was far too forbidding for me to feel comfortable with,' recalls Hema.

Her next tutor was Sikkil Ramaswamy Pillai of Triveni Kala Sangam in Delhi. 'He was a kind old man and in a way my first guru. His other disciple at that time was the then Miss India, Indrani Rehman, a very beautiful lady and a very fine dancer too. In fact, I have spent many evenings just watching Indrani practise with our guru. It was a treat watching her move as gracefully as she did.' Hema was content learning from Ramaswamy Pillai except that he had a peculiar problem. When accompanying Hema on her dance shows, Pillai would on stage break into singing rather than concentrate on his *nattuvangam* (beats of the dance). This was embarrassing for the professional singers on the stage because Pillai was not exactly a great singer. Under these circumstances, Jaya had no option but to replace him with another teacher.

She briefly trained under teachers like Thiruvalaputhur Swaminatha Pillai, Mylapore Gauri Ammal and Arunachalam Pillai. The irony was that all of them delivered their best but somehow they failed to measure up to Jaya's exacting standards.

In her later years, Hema learnt Kuchipudi from Guru Vempatti Chinna Satyam, and Mohini Attam from Guru Natanam Gopal Krishnan.

The frequent change of tutors disturbed Hema. It was annoying for her to get accustomed to a new temperament and a new pattern every time. Jaya understood her discomfort but it was a small price for the bigger dream she envisaged for her daughter. The family trusted Jaya's wisdom and supported her wholeheartedly. She nurtured a deep regard for the ancient tradition, its mythological and social origin. Bharatanatyam was originally performed at the temples and it was only in the late 1930s, because of the tireless efforts of Rukminidevi Arundale (founder of Kalakshetra), that it finally found recognition as a performing art. Jaya diligently read the *Natyashastra* and consciously worked at Hema imbibing both *natya* and *abhinaya* in her portrayal. In time to come Jaya convinced her husband that the spark she saw in her daughter could be fanned into a blazing talent only if the family shifted to Madras.

The decision involved Chakravarti seeking a transfer from ESIC and uprooting his two sons. Kannan was studying science at Delhi's Hansraj College while younger Jagannath was completing his schooling from Madrasi Higher Secondary School. After a lot of deliberation, Chakravarti took the tough decision to migrate, initially just with his wife and daughter while the two boys stayed back with their maternal grandmother.

It was the summer of 1962 when the Chakravartis shifted bag and baggage to make a home out of Madras. Hema was admitted in her new school, Rosary Matriculation. But over a period of time as her travelling for her dance performances increased, Hema found it difficult to cope with her studies and dance so Chakravarti shifted her to a new course, Andhra Matriculation, which is equivalent to the correspondence course of present times.

In Madras, once again, their quest for the right guru continued. Jaya contacted several tutors but somehow, something was always amiss. Only a very few met up with their expectations. Hema attributes her strong foundation in classical dance to her three gurus – Guru Kittappa Pillai from whom she learnt Bharatanatyam; Guru Vempatti Chinna Satyam from whom she learnt Kuchipudi, and to Guru Natanam Gopal Krishnan from whom she learnt Mohini Attam. She met Guru Kittappa Pillai by chance when attending a dance performance of Vyjayanthimala. The family was thoroughly impressed by her pure classical performance and made it a point to meet the great teacher backstage. 'It was a great day for us when Guru Kittappa Pillai came to our home and agreed to teach me. He was a very affectionate and a friendly person and I thoroughly enjoyed learning dance from him.'

Thus began a new phase of Hema learning a deeper and concentrated form of Bharatanatyam. And for the first time in several years Jaya did not feel the need to replace him. Finally, her search for the perfect guru was over. Kittappa Pillai continued to teach Hema all through his life till he passed away a decade ago. 'As guru-shishya, we were so well synchronized that as long as he lived, I did not feel the need to seek knowledge elsewhere. Meeting him also made me aware that just in the way a disciple hankers for the right guru, similarly, the guru is always in search of a deserving disciple to whom he can impart his knowledge. This is true of both, the spiritual as well as the dance guru. Strange are the ways of life that often we spend a lifetime looking for a guru and never find one. I was fortunate to find both, my dance guru Kittappa Pillai and many years later, my spiritual guru Ma Indiraji at a point in my life when I needed them the most.'

Interestingly, film producers started approaching Hema when she was barely fourteen. It is a common practice for filmmakers to pick up stage artistes and give them a break in films, and since Hema was considerably well known in the circle, she was frequently wooed by those connected in show business. Her first offer to do a dance item in a Tamil film came from producer Vellu Mani followed by another dance item for a Telugu film. 'As children we were seldom taken to cinema halls. Nor did my parents ever visit them. Except AIFACS Hall situated a little away from our home in Connaught Place. It was a dainty theatre that screened children's films and Appa took us there on Sunday mornings. After the film, we usually had lunch at a nearby Udipi restaurant. The food was more or less similar to what we ate at home but there was a difference in the presentation and that was very attractive. Also, this was the only time my brothers and I were allowed to have a Coke instead of the usual coffee.

'Besides AIFACS there was Regal Cinema which too was in Connaught Place. The first film I remember watching there, was Vyjayanthimala's *Nagin*. I enjoyed it because the film had good music and dance. A few years later, while I was returning from school, I saw the poster of *Hariyali Aur Raasta* outside the same theatre. I pestered Amma to take me to the film but she wasn't keen. When I insisted she sent my brother with me. I did not quite follow the story. All I remember about it was a weeping heroine

Hema rehearsing for a dance photo shoot.

who made everyone in the audience feel extremely sad … After that I never visited a cinema hall again until I joined films. The only entertainment encouraged by the family was music and dance concerts.'

Jaya wanted her daughter to become a dancer. She had never dreamt of a career in films for her, but destiny had different plans.

By this time both Kannan and Jagan had completed their college and joined the family in Madras. Jagan was pursuing a degree in law while Kannan was employed as a college lecturer.

Barely fourteen, Hema started getting offers from Tamil film producers to launch her as a heroine.

The brothers were spreading their wings but remained connected with the changes in their little sister's life.

One day, a Tamil film producer arrived at the Chakravarti residence with a proposal to launch Hema as a heroine. Chakravarti was not enticed by the offer and rejected the idea outright. Jaya suggested, however, that there was no harm in exploring the possibilities. She was ignorant about the film world but had friends closely connected to the medium and sought their opinion. They seemed positive and informed her that the concerned producer was a big name in Tamil films. Chakravarti tried dissuading his wife but she assured him that they would not plunge into any decision unless completely convinced of the offer. 'Appa was not in favour of my working in the films but Amma had the knack of having her way. To be honest, I too was not keen at all but she assured me that if I was uncomfortable I could opt out after completing this one film. Young as I was, Amma respected my freedom of choice. That was a big consolation,' she recalls about her first film offer.

The producer made a grand announcement and spoke in glorious terms about his two heroines, Hema and J. Jayalalitha – who went on to become chief minister of Tamil Nadu. On his suggestion Jaya Chakravarti agreed to change Hema's name to Sujata because the producer felt Hema Malini was not an appropriate name for a film heroine. 'Though disappointed, Amma agreed trusting his better judgement,' says Hema. 'Looking back, that was the first compromise on our instincts. Here was a name my mother had so painstakingly chosen for me and the entire family approved of, so who was this stranger to disregard our decision … ?'

The shooting for the film began soon after the press announcements. The two heroines were draped in elaborate costumes and made to wear funny wigs. 'I looked and felt hideous dressed in *pavadai davani,* a half sari, but of course, nobody asked for my opinion and I was used to keeping quiet,' shares Hema reticently.

But deep within her, there was a growing fear. Hema was at an awkward age and with all that was happening around her, she found herself retreating into a shell.

Then, a few months after the first schedule of the laborious shooting in Madurai, the Chakravartis read in the newspapers that the producer had dropped Hema from the project and replaced her with someone else … 'It was a rude shock and I felt as if someone had struck me hard on the face. It was not as if we had been pestering him to take me in his project, so how could he unceremoniously drop me without even an explanation?' While venting her anger Hema reveals that she was secretly relieved to be out of the mess. It was the manner in which it was done that was humiliating. 'I felt rejected and my mother felt insulted. It was not as if we had gone seeking for a role. He had made the overture and now suddenly, had thrown me out of the film. "She does not have the making of a star", he had declared in print. I felt crushed, but after a brief period of mourning was able to rise above my suffering. But not my mother! A strong-willed woman, her pride could not swallow the condemnation …

'I can never forget my mother's pained expression of those days,' says Hema. Jaya went through her normal routine but there was a desolation she could not rise above. Hema would often find her sitting all by herself lost in thought. Even though Hema was very young, she sensed what her mother was going through. 'I was her most cherished possession and she couldn't accept a stranger dismissing me so casually,' Hema recalls emotionally.

Jaya's deep anguish and sudden isolation instilled a resolution in Hema. 'It is my firm belief that whenever you challenge somebody, the person always rises to the occasion.' Hema was determined to take up the challenge and restore her mother's self-worth. One evening, as Jaya sat depressed looking out of the window, Hema went up to her and said awkwardly, 'I'll become an actress … I'll work in films … I'll do what you say and succeed.' That was the turning point!

Says Hema, 'This may sound unreal but that was the first time I had a direct dialogue with Lord Krishna. I told Him, "You have brought me to this situation and now it is up to you to ride me through this humiliation. You have to make me worthy of the challenges thrown at me." I had implored and cried to Him to make me strong and powerful. It was total surrender and God listened to my prayers. Nobody would believe this but things began looking up soon after that, almost within the next few days.'

Hema's godfather Anantha Swamy walked into their lives out of the blue. It was as if his entry coincided with the infamous producer's exit. Destiny was playing its cards for the Chakravartis and they had to merely toe the line. The following events occurred so rapidly that there was no time for reflection.

Anantha Swamy spotted Hema Malini for the first time at a dance concert organized by the Chakravartis' family friend, K. Subramanium, a prominent film producer and father of the erstwhile Bharatanatyam dancer Padma Subramanium. Subramanium was a staunch supporter of new talent. He organized a special dance recital of Hema at his residence to introduce her to various dance organizations and critics. It was a hugely successful show after which Hema came to be recognized as 'Delhi Hema Malini' (since there was another dancer of the same name in Madras) amongst dance organizations.

Impressed by her performance, Anantha Swamy visited the Chakravartis and informed them that he was making a Hindi film, and asked whether Hema would be interested to work as a heroine opposite Hindi cinema's superstar Raj Kapoor. While Jaya and Chakravarti appeared at loss for words, Hema, without consulting her parents promptly replied yes. Anantha Swamy was taken aback by her bravado but did not show it. When he left, the family wondered if he was a con man taking them for a ride. But when Anantha Swamy reappeared a few days later with three air tickets to fly them to Bombay to meet the showman, his credentials were no longer suspect. Hema says, 'He made it clear from the beginning that Raj Kapoor would be the one to be taking the decision. We had no objection and when it was time to travel, Amma and my brother Jagannath accompanied me. It was our first journey to Bombay and that too by air! My brother and I were too excited to contain ourselves.'

A South Indian producer had signed bulk dates with Raj Kapoor and was keen to launch a film immediately. This was in the wake of his blockbuster *Sangam,* so his heroine had to be someone beautiful and also an accomplished dancer, in short a substitute for Raj Kapoor's earlier heroine Vyjayanthimala. At first glance Hema Malini fitted the bill but the approval could come only after a screen test.

The screen test was conducted at R.K. Studio in Deonar and Hema was understandably very nervous. Led into a large make-up room, Hema and her mother stood self-consciously while her personal staff comprising make-up man Madhav Pai, dressman Vishnu, and spot-boy Hanuman assumed total responsibility. Being veterans in their fields, they felt protective of the debutante. Vishnu took her to the dress room displaying different film costumes worn by legendary stars like Padmini and Vyjayanthimala, adding, 'One day your costumes too will be hung up besides these.' Hema feels nostalgic about their purity of affection. She says while doing her make-up, Madhav dada gently inspired her confidence to prepare for the test shot. He said, 'Be unafraid, perform as if there is no one in the room except you … Open your heart and see how the lights shine on your face.' With these comforting words, the anxieties abated momentarily but fear resurfaced as she walked to the sets to take position. Raj Kapoor was behind the camera and he was so reassuring that Hema lost all her inhibitions. 'Rajji was so gentle, so casual that it was almost as if the camera did not exist.' Shot over, Raj Kapoor turned to director K. Asif and music director Shankar present in the studio and said, 'She is going to be the biggest star of the Indian screen.' After the caustic remark from the last producer, this was like balm to Hema and her mother's festering wounds.

Jaya Chakravarti agreed to the contract, oblivious of Raj Kapoor's superstar stature. 'We were ignorant about Hindi films and his position. What mattered to us was that the producer from the South ought to be taught a lesson,' asserts Hema. 'I had no serious ambitions of a long-term career in acting. I thought I'd do one or two films and then quit. I am not sure what went on in my mother's mind, but after signing *Sapno Ka Saudagar*, she seemed to be at peace with herself.'

With the contract neatly tucked in their bag, Hema and Jaya returned to Madras. It had not dawned on them until then that they would soon be shifting, once again, to a new city. Perhaps Jaya sensed it, but did not mention it for fear of upsetting her husband. No decision was ever implemented at home without his consent, but it is to Chakravarti's credit that he always took his wife's views into account.

'My father was not too pleased with our decision and made his displeasure apparent. This created a lot of tension in the family. To protest, Appa stopped having meals at home and this distressed Amma. Then one fine day, suddenly he called a truce and joined the family for supper. I still don't know how they resolved the conflict but we were given the go-ahead … ' says Hema, her eyes shining.

It was not as if Chakravarti was not supportive of his wife. He was encouraging of Hema learning dance and actively participated in her shows by introducing the dance items and the performers, a tradition followed by his older son Kannan today. 'There was a clear division of duties between my parents regarding my dance shows,' remembers Hema, 'Appa coordinated with the theatre, the orchestra and dramatically introduced the items researched from various sources, while it was Amma's duty to dress me up and draw an itinerary for the show. Both of them were always in the wings when I was on stage – Amma watching my every step and Appa, the expressions of the audience. His face brimmed with joy every time someone praised me. It's just that he was not comfortable with the idea of me working in films. His main concern in those days was what his office colleagues would say. It is possible that nobody said anything but it was a sensitive issue with him and as a family we respected his anxieties.'

Chakravarti was riding a busy phase in his career and observed irregular hours at home during a specific season of the year. The family was trained not to disturb him during these

Hema Malini with screen legend Raj Kapoor in a still from her first Hindi film Sapno Ka Saudagar.

stressful months. But gradually, some rules were changing. Jaya needed to accompany Hema on her frequent visits to Bombay. This made Chakravarti edgy though he tried not to show it. It was not easy for Jaya to find her bearings with a young daughter in an alien city. Or for Hema being put to test once again. After her last bitter experience with the Tamil film industry, Hema was comparatively less shy though still awkward. 'I was very tall and very thin and unlike present times being slim was not considered sexy.' The Hindi film producer was relieved to discover that she was familiar with the language, even if she spoke with an accent, which was understandable. On the first day of shooting, director Mahesh Kaul deliberately restricted Hema's scenes to a minimum without any dialogues. It was his way of getting her acquainted with her surroundings, her costume and her character. Hema played a gypsy girl in the film.

On the second day, however, Hema discovered that film shooting is no child's play. She had to perform a tongue-lashing scene with Raj Kapoor where she flings herself on him like a wild cat mouthing long native dialogues. Provided with the lines the previous evening, Hema was well prepared but the director wanted her to emote while jerking her shoulder, and she was unable to combine the gesture with the dialogues. There were fourteen retakes and with every 'One more' from the director, Hema's self-confidence diminished. From the corner of her eyes she watched Anantha Swamy stare at the cameraman feeling guilty about the waste of raw stock. She could sense her mother's rising tension and the exasperation of her director. Feeling miserable, Hema in between shots whispered to her mother in Tamil that she didn't wish to do the film, and asked if they could quit and go home. Jaya scolded her for her foolish thoughts and urged her instead to concentrate on the director's instructions, 'Why can't you grasp what he says. It's not that difficult.'

Something resolved for Hema that very moment and the fifteenth take was okayed! Everyone on the sets heaved a sigh of relief. Hema felt close to breaking down but held back her tears, sat quietly in a corner when the director called her by his side. Her heart sank, could this mean that the shot was not okay and he wanted one more take. Mahesh Kaul smiled, picked out a rose from a vase and held it to Hema. 'Watch this flower and observe the emotions it arouses within you – you will react differently to it when you are happy and differently when sad. Acting calls for observing your emotions minutely and projecting them for camera.' Hema says that other actors might have gone to acting schools but she has learnt it first-hand on the sets from her director. 'Mahesh Kaul was my acting guru and all the acting I did in the forthcoming scenes was demonstrated by him. He was a tough teacher and no matter how long it took to get the shot right, he did not give up till completely satisfied. And this applied not just to me but also to my co-stars. There were times he was extremely curt and times when he was extremely gentle. Whenever he found me struggling and confused he would explain the scene to me like one does to a child and suddenly after that it became so simple,' says a wonderstruck Hema. As the film progressed, the producer hired a maulvi to teach her Urdu to cultivate a better accent. And Hema thoroughly enjoyed learning the nuances of this beautiful language.

In Jaya's absence Chakravarti assumed undivided responsibility at home. And so did the boys. Hema's younger brother Jagan suddenly stopped playing the tease. 'This was unsettling for me … ' expresses Hema. 'I missed my explosive moments with Jagan when he would tear my music and dance books (where I wrote the *jati*), and to take revenge I would empty a pot of ink on his face and then run away so that Amma wouldn't spank me. Suddenly, those innocent moments disappeared from my life. Whenever I returned from my long stints of shooting in Bombay, the first thing that I did was to rush to my room and check if my *jati* books were in order. They were untouched. It was the beginning of a new phase in my life.'

The innocent, carefree moments of life disappeared when Hema moved to Bombay with her mother. It was the beginning of a new phase in her life.

The Scent of Stardom

Jagan was confused with the sudden changes of abode. He felt uprooted because his mother now spent all her time accompanying Hema and it was something the other siblings were not accustomed to. It was an anxious phase for all of them but soon, the family got used to the constant references to the world of cinema. Jaya now discussed finding accommodation, transport, monthly expenses and a budget for Hema's new wardrobe openly with Chakravarti. She would neatly jot down in her notebook the names and addresses of friends and acquaintances they knew in Bombay. 'It will come in handy,' she would say philosophically.

As the big day to take off for Bombay approached, both mother and daughter appeared nervous. It was not easy to disconnect from the memories of the present home, from the family. They were required to be for long shoots in Bombay's claustrophobic studios and looked forward to being back with the family.

There was a different fragrance in the air when Jaya returned home. Chakravarti and his sons blossomed in her presence. Jaya pampered them by cooking their favourite meals, served over

Facing Page: *Films and more films broke Hema's inhibitions to perform in front of the camera. Hema in a still from* Sharafat.

stories of Bombay's film world. 'My parents were poles apart and yet completely in sync,' recalls Hema, 'What bonded them together was their love for art and music … Appa had a deep understanding of dance and drama but he seldom expressed himself. Amma was spontaneous and adventurous. Once she set out to do something, no power in the world could dissuade her.' It was Jaya's conviction that eventually motivated the family to migrate to Bombay.

Initially, Hema and her mother moved into Hema's mentor Anantha Swamy's home in the city's eastern suburb of Chembur. They stayed with Anantha Swamy's family for about a year. 'To be fair to them, they were good hosts, but it is never practical to live with anyone for too long. So after a year, as I signed more films and began shooting regularly, we rented a flat in Bandra and moved out.' The first apartment that they rented was in a skyscraper in Bombay's mid-town Malabar Hill. It was a prestigious locality but somehow Hema and her mother were uncomfortable in their new surrounding.

'All my growing-up years I had lived on ground level and felt ill at ease watching sunrise from the top floor. It was a beautiful view of cars speeding by, but it also reminded you that Bombay was full of people but none to call your own … When you are used to a large family, it is difficult to survive without them. Even if one member of the family is away, the house looks deserted. The family had never been separated before this and I missed being with my brothers. The day passed in the hot studios, but when dusk fell, it was lonely with just my mother and I in an alien city. Appa visited us from time to time. He sensed we were uneasy in our rented flat and began looking for a bungalow in the western suburbs. As soon as he located an appropriate house in Juhu, we moved out.'

The new home was a strange mix of their Delhi and Madras homes. There was sufficient greenery around the house and most importantly, it was on the ground floor. 'On my way to the studios and back home, I had to drive past Juhu Chowpatty and I loved watching the sea ... I loved the smell of the beach and those days the sand and the water were of a different colour ... golden sand and deep green sea.'

Over a period of time as Hema got established in Bombay, her brothers and her father joined them there for good. Unaffected by the buzz she created in the film studios and cinema halls, life in the Chakravarti household remained amazingly normal. Their day began with the routine puja and ended with a vegetarian dinner eaten by the family together. Chakravarti was the patriarch of the family and followed everyone's dreams.

He had high expectations from his sons and now that his daughter was well immersed in an artistic career, he expected some form of excellence from Hema as well. 'Appa had been a hard-working professional all through his career and expected the same from his children. My debut film had not fared well at the box office but for some strange reason, I was offered many films and all these films were successful. I don't know why but nobody seemed to mourn the failure of *Sapno Ka Saudagar.* Not Raj Kapoor, not my producers and certainly not me because I was oblivious of the box office expectations.'

As luck would have it all the top banners signed up Hema for their films. She did Madan Mohla's *Sharafat* and Vijay Anand's *Johnny Mera Naam*, both big hits. 'Asitda always relied on the story rather than his technical skills. Emotion was the scoring point in all his films,' she reveals. About *Johnny Mera Naam,* she says, it was the right film at the right time with the right cast. Dev Anand and she starred in eight films together after *Johnny Mera Naam* released in 1970. *Tere Mere Sapne* in 1971, *Shareef Badmash*, *Chupa Rustam* and *Joshila* in 1973, *Amir Garib* in 1974, *Jaaneman* in 1976, *Sachche Ka Bol Bala* in 1989 and decades later *Censor* in 2001, but somehow none could match the magic of *Johnny Mera Naam.*

Johnny Mera Naam's memorable song '*O mere raja ...* ' was shot in a sky trolley at Rajgir situated 100 kms south-east of Patna. The actors had to travel by the ropeway, the only mode of transport to reach the location, the Buddhist temple situated on the other side of the mountain. On the way, director Vijay Anand spontaneously decided to shoot a few lines on the ropeway too. For a compact frame, he made Hema sit on Dev Anand's lap. The distance to the destination was only a few minutes, but a prankster on location, switched off the current. The trolley came to a halt and the pair was stranded in mid-air. Hema, who has an inherent fear of heights, was petrified. To distract her, Dev Anand entertained his leading lady with jokes. Soon the culprit was caught, and the trolley restarted. Says Hema, 'Even today, when I see the film, the fear of that scene returns … It's funny how memories associated with movies come rushing when you see an old clipping or a photograph.'

As Hema's career started flourishing, her caretaker Anantha Swamy began to feel threatened and to impose his presence began holding back information from the mother and daughter. Jaya was concerned about his unreasonable behaviour but the relationship could not be severed because they were bound by a contract. They had signed important documents without questioning and now there was no way out. Initially, Jaya left Hema out of the brewing tension, but soon the pressures became too much for her to handle single-handedly. Writers and directors complained that they were denied access to Hema, and Jaya was completely in the dark about Hema's payments and shooting schedules.

'One day, my mother and he were in the midst of an angry discussion. The argument was not leading anywhere. Exasperated, Amma just snatched the contract papers from Anantha Swamy's hand and tore them to pieces. He had not expected this from her. Neither had she. Amma had reacted under extreme pressure. She was like a tigress protecting her cub. Suddenly the bond that had seemed like life-long had snapped! My mother and I were free. It was a euphoric moment and perhaps that was the only way it could have happened.'

The ensuing legal proceedings left a deep scar on all three of them. For days none of them could muster courage to discuss the repercussions. The media played up the drama and splashed it as headlines on the front page, but since none of them retaliated, the controversy died a natural death. Today Hema would rather let bygones be bygones. 'We parted without grudges and I

A still from Hema Malini's biggest hit with Dev Anand, Johnny Mera Naam.

The reigning queen of Hindi cinema: Success came with a lot of hard work and commitment.

maintain that Anantha Swamy was a good-hearted man and had it not been for him, I would not have been in films,' she declares with finality.

In Anantha Swamy's absence it was time for Jaya to assume a new avtaar and take charge of her daughter's career. She now personally supervised Hema's dates and payments. It was a new role for both of them that sometimes led to disputes because Jaya committed dates to a certain producer while Hema wanted to favour another. But these were trivial matters usually resolved amicably. Hema says that despite the frequent highs and lows in her career and life, her relationship with her mother remained consistent till the end, 'She was my source of comfort, my anchor and in a strange way, my goal.'

While they stayed in the bungalow in Juhu, Chakravarti had wisely invested his daughter's earnings in a vast property on the 12th Road of Juhu Vile Parle Development Scheme, a three-storeyed bungalow. It was just the kind of home Chakravarti had envisioned for his daughter. Situated in a quiet lane festooned with gulmohar trees, there was a huge garden stretching across the boundary wall of the bungalow. The three floors had sufficient rooms to accommodate a large family (and in time to come, some members of Jaya Chakravarti's maiden family as well). All the bedrooms were located upstairs while the ground floor comprised the kitchen, dining area, office and living room made up in two sections.

Every morning, filmmakers flocked to the house to sign Hema and waited endlessly to make a proposal. Everyone knew that Hema left for shooting at nine in the morning. At about quarter to nine it was a routine for her make-up man and hairdresser to come down with her paraphernalia and settle in the car. Between nine and quarter past nine, Hema descended the staircase, walked past the room without a glance in anyone's direction straight to the verandah and entered her car. The same producers returned day after day until the lovely lady gave her nod to the project.

She was the reigning queen of Hindi cinema and almost all the leading heroes of that time, Dharmendra, Jeetendra, Sanjeev Kumar to name a few, held a torch for the dazzling beauty. Sometimes there were innocent episodes on the sets when the co-star could not contain his attraction and openly flirted with her. Sometimes confessions were subtler, expressed via scribbled notes and eye contact. At times there were messages sent through Hema's personal staff, make-up man and hairdresser and on a couple of occasions there were serious proposals carried over by family members or colleagues. Chakravarti strongly disapproved of the entire bunch of proposers. He made no efforts to hide his deep contempt and prejudice against North Indian film heroes. And there was a reason for this.

Chakravarti and Jaya were deeply affected by the stories doing the rounds on the grapevine about lead star Vyjayanthimala. Here was an ideal Iyengar actress they looked up to and modelled their daughter's career on, but were devastated by her alleged involvement with her North Indian co-star. Hema's parents did not want history repeating itself with their daughter.

Most women in Hema's position would have basked and blossomed with the overwhelming male attention she received. But Hema was terrified at the havoc all the romantic propositions created in her life. 'I had fame and money, but no peace of mind. I was shooting round the clock and life was moving too fast for me to pause and ponder,' she harks back. The rapid changes in Hema's career evoked mixed emotions in her parents, and Jaya in her overprotection resented Hema's proximity with anyone outside the immediate family.

On the sets, if the hero got friendly with Hema, Jaya made her displeasure quite apparent. She was present at all her shoots and on days she was shooting intimate scenes, directors dreaded Jaya's visits to their sets. 'It got claustrophobic beyond a point, I agree, but it was self-designed. I had grown up without ever knowing my private space and did not know how to negotiate for it after all these years. Other actresses kept secrets, but I could not. It had become my habit to share everything with Amma.' In the middle of a shot if Hema caught her mother looking stern, she would immediately stiffen. The directors got frustrated, coaxed Hema to infuse more emotion in the scenes, and behind her back, probably grumbled.

Jaya continued with her strict surveillance. Filmmakers found it impossible to persuade Hema to embrace her hero passionately. As soon as the actor drew closer, she retreated. The film magazines labelled her '*thandi*' Malini and the heroes called her an 'ice maiden' but Hema never contradicted them. 'They were entitled to their opinion about me. The truth was that I wanted to mingle with the rest of the unit but no matter how hard I tried, I just could not drop my guard. I hoped that others would sense my reserve and draw me into the crowd, but people stayed away intimidated by my stardom,' Hema reflects.

They say that Hema Malini saw Dharmendra for the first time at a film premiere in 1969. Both agree that it was attraction at first sight. Dharmendra is said to have whispered '*Kudi changi hai*' (Nice girl!) to Shashi Kapoor sitting beside him. Hema who understood a few words of Punjabi blushed silently. It was a coincidence that the two signed four films together in the same year of which *Tum Haseen Main Jawan* released in 1970, *Naya Zamana* in 1971, *Raja Jaani* and *Sharafat* in 1972.

Cupid struck his arrow fiercely and on the sets of *Seeta Aur Geeta,* director Ramesh Sippy was the common confidante. What endeared Hema to Dharmendra, he says was her beauty and simplicity, while Hema confessed that she felt reassured in Dharmendra's presence. Not many know this, but Hema was not the original choice for *Seeta Aur Geeta.* The role was first offered to Mumtaz who could not accept the film due to non-availability of dates. Then Ramesh Sippy approached Hema but she was not sure if she would be able to carry off the double role. 'The sober role was easy but doing comedy is always tough. It required me to do a lot of ridiculous things like walking on a rope, high jumps, and even sit on a ceiling fan. Every time I had to do these acrobatics, I would insist that Rameshji demonstrate it to me. So

Hema Malini and Dharmendra: The perfect pair of the Hindi cinema in a still from Tum Haseen Main Jawan.

he would climb onto a ladder, sit on the blades of the fan and flap his legs. In all these scenes I have literally copied him,' she relates with a smile.

Two years later during the shooting of *Sholay* the chemistry between the lead pair was palpable to everyone on the sets. Both were extremely attractive and successful. He was Hindi cinema's reigning star. She was the country's most eligible beauty. The film took a long time to be completed. During the location shoot in Bangalore, it is said that Dharmendra begged of the light-men to do errors in the shot so that he could embrace his heroine again and again. Similar stories about their blooming romance were making the rounds from their other shooting locations as well, and hell broke loose in Hema's home.

As Hema's affection for Dharmendra strengthened, it led to a lot of strain in her relationship with her family. Her father and brothers were openly opposed to any overture made by Hema's dashing Jat hero. Jaya Chakravarti was less demonstrative. Deep down she echoed her husband's anxieties but never expressed these to avoid tensions. But tempers flared up every time intimate stories involving Hema appeared in print. Then, Chakravarti confronted Jaya and she had much explaining to do in defence of her daughter. The confrontations took a toll on her physical and mental health. Call it providence but Jaya's youngest sister Shanta suffering from a broken marriage returned to her parents around this time. On Jaya's request Chakravarti persuaded Shanta to come and live with them and be a constant companion to Hema. The decision proved cathartic for both the aunt and the niece. For the first time Hema discovered her soulmate, and Shanta in her new surroundings, gradually buried her old wounds. But most important, the new arrangement provided Jaya with the much-needed respite.

Jaya took the crucial decision to stop accompanying Hema for her shootings and now stayed at home sorting out Hema's dates with producers, while Shanta began escorting Hema everywhere. But it was not that easy for Jaya to disconnect with her daughter. So, after finishing her morning routine, she would drop by at the shootings during the day. When she did not, she insisted that Hema come home for lunch.

Hema resented the invasion on her time but could not disobey her mother even though it inconvenienced everybody. The entire exercise was a nightmare. Shootings were invariably held up and producers disapproved of this collossal waste of time. The extended lunch-break inevitably led to delay in pack-up, which infuriated the hero. Hema expected her mother to understand the complications and stop making demands on her, but Jaya was going through a turbulent phase and needed reassurance. Alienated from her daughter's routine she experienced a loss of identity and exploded at the slightest provocation. Hema could not fathom her extreme responses and dreaded being interrogated as soon as she got home.

Jaya suspected Hema spent her time elsewhere after pack-up. Hema felt offended having to explain herself all the time. One late evening, Hema had just returned home from shooting. She was in her room upstairs, removing her make-up, when Jaya walked in with her usual questions. Something just snapped inside Hema. Sitting down in a chair, she informed her quietly that she had decided to quit films. 'I told her I could no longer cope with the accusations and the pressures. This was the first time I had spoken to her as an adult and I could see that she was deeply hurt. But time had come for me to take a stand. I reminded her that I had joined films to pursue her dream. Now, it was her choice whether I should quit or accomplish that goal. That's when the seriousness dawned on her and she withdrew ... Today, I understand her perspective better than I did then. It was not easy for her to let go of her special child, one she had protected so fiercely. It was not easy for me either, but the umbilical chord had to be snapped. Perhaps, that is the fate of stardom. At some point, the closest ties have to be severed because the rocket has to ascend solo,' she sighs.

The isolation hurt Jaya and understandably so. Left to defending Hema all the time to the family and to the rest of the world, Jaya felt weighed down with unexpressed worries. The only one she never rebelled against was Chakravarti. She trusted his decisions wholeheartedly. Reminisces Hema, 'I was in my mid-twenties and Appa had grown anxious about my marriage. He would bring photographs of prospective grooms for my approval. I would look at them indifferently and return them without a word. "What do you think?" my father would ask. I had no answer …

'I was attracted to Dharamji but did not have the courage to say so. I had the better sense to realize that it was a futile relationship, him being a married man, but due to our exceptional circumstances could not sever the ties. What began as an innocent friendship on the sets, steadily turned into an attachment. He made me laugh and feel good about myself. I was

Attracted to Dharmendra, Hema was hesitant to talk about her feelings. Just being with him made her happy and feel good about herself. Seen here in a still from Hum Tere Aashiq Hain.

always happy when he was around. Circumstances compelled us to be together all the time because we were doing many films together,' says Hema wistfully.

They made a phenomenal pair and filmmakers loved casting them together. Pramod Chakraborty did four (*Naya Zamana, Jugnu, Dream Girl* and *Azaad*) and Dulal Guha did three (*Dost, Pratigya* and *Dil Ka Hira*) films with this hit pair. The other directors who cast the pair were Ramanand Sagar in *Charas*, M.A. Thirumugam in *Maa*, Manmohan Desai in *Chacha Bhatija,* Ravi Chopra in *The Burning Train,* Basu Chatterji in *Dillagi,* Mohan Sehgal in *Raja Jaani* and *Samrat,* Harmesh Malhotra in *Patthar Aur Payal,* Umesh Mehra in *Alibaba Aur 40 Chor* and Biswajeet Chatterjee in *Kehte Hai Mujhko Raja.* There was a magical chemistry about their pairing and the audience was completely mesmerized by them.

Then, one day while they were in the middle of a shot, Dharmendra asked her, 'Do you love me?'

'I was taken aback and did not answer at once. Then I said, "I will only love the person I marry." He persisted, "That's not an answer," to which I replied, "Yes, this is my answer,"' Hema rewinds to their whirlwind courtship days.

It was the most talked-about relationship. Gossip magazines were full of vicious stories that destroyed their peace at home. The constant attacks in print affected all of them. Hema's parents were accused of dominating their daughter, and Dharmendra of deliberately keeping his family away from the limelight. In the many years that followed nobody ever saw Dharmendra's wife, Prakash accompanying her husband at any public functions except close family gatherings. The negative publicity was embarrassing for everyone involved. Chakravarti worried excessively about the inordinate delay in Hema's marriage and began consulting astrologers.

Around this time Hema was scheduled to leave for a long outdoor stint to Malta for *Charas* with Dharmendra. 'My father was adamant about accompanying me for the shoot, something he had never done earlier,' says Hema. She looked forward to leaving the city because it was a break from the prying media and the brewing tensions at home.

In Malta there were different kinds of pressures to be dealt with. Chakravarti was all the time watching over Hema's hero and disapproved of any physical or social contact with his daughter. Those days film stars travelled from the hotel to the location in a common car. Chakravarti disapproved of this because it meant sharing a vehicle with Hema's co-star Dharmendra. He made sure to keep the two apart. 'When we would get into the car, he would warn me in Tamil to take the corner seat and plant himself beside me. But Dharamji was always one up on Appa. Using some excuse or the other, he would, at the last moment, open the door by my side, push me to the middle and snuggle in beside me … Today, one can laugh over such childishness but at that time it was not so amusing. I was caught between the two men I loved dearly and there was nothing I could do to make peace between them,' she recalls with a shrug.

Interestingly, Chakravarti had no serious objection to Dharmendra except for the fact that he loved his daughter. In fact, in less guarded moments, when they were not opposing each other, the two got along famously. In between shots, Hema often caught them chatting with each other and wished they could be that way always. It was unfortunate because everyone in the Chakravarti family approved of Dharmendra, but not as a son-in-law and for obvious reasons …

In the meantime Hema's brothers had settled down with good jobs. Kannan had joined the State Bank of India as a staff officer and moved to Calcutta. He was married to Prabha, an Iyengar girl chosen by the family, while Jagannath had joined The New India Insurance in Bombay and married his Gujarati colleague, Smita. The only worry in the family was now about Hema's single status and this was becoming an increasingly sensitive topic. Jaya Chakravarti made it her mission to find a suitable match for her daughter. She signed writer-director Girish

Karnad in two of her productions (*Swami* and *Ratnadeep*) because she felt he was a worthy suitor for her gorgeous daughter. That was also the reason she encouraged newcomer Dheeraj Kumar as an actor and later as a producer, but Hema was not similarly inclined and Jaya's plans fizzled out.

The superstar emoting in romantic songs and sequences all through the day on the sets, after pack-up was left wondering about her own personal love story. In retrospect Hema feels that Hindi cinema, in order to sell dreams, overemphasizes on love to an extent that those not in love feel they are missing out on something. Like all girls her age Hema fantasized an image of her dream man and unknowingly Dharmendra fitted the bill. The attraction was mutual and in the surroundings they worked in, the reasons for attachment were plenty.

'I tried turning away from Dharamji but I just could not. There was something inherently good about the human being that made it difficult for me to break the bond,' says Hema. Her family hoped that her attraction was just a passing phase and she would get over him, but time drew them only closer. Hema was unable to express herself to her family. 'I don't know how many people will believe this but I never thought of marrying him. Even now, I don't say that what happened was the best option. Nobody calculatedly falls in love. It just happens! Whenever I thought about my life partner, I always imagined someone like him – handsome, strong, with a peaceful face, but never him. It was, however destined that it had to be him … We never made promises … never discussed the future … or planned anything permanent. In fact we did not go through a conventional courtship. He may have been a flirt, but he did not flirt with me. Nor did I. I did not know how to flirt. I just knew that being with him, talking to him made me happy. And happiness was all I wanted. My intention was never to cause suffering to anyone,' she confesses candidly.

Passion and Protest

A daughter who always admired and respected her parents, though never wanted to hurt anybody had unconsciously pained her father. Chakravarti preoccupied himself in various ways, read for long hours, spent time with his family but his heart ached for his daughter. Hema says that he started the dance institute, Natyavihar Kala Kendra in Madras only to distract himself from his anxieties, and it was not part of the original scheme of things.

Some years ago when Chakravarti invested his daughter's earnings in the Juhu bungalow, he had also bought another sprawling property on the Kasturi Ranga Road in Madras, where he intended to build a dream bungalow for his daughter. In time to come he was so excited about the project that he shifted to Madras to personally supervise the construction. The site workers were accustomed to Chakravarti watching over them all through summer and in the rains standing under his umbrella.

During the process he spent many lonely months in Madras away from the family. To make sure he used his time productively, Chakravarti engaged himself in two passionate projects. The first, a tribute to his late father Srisaila Chakravarti, an erudite scholar

***Facing page:** Hema and Dharmendra in* Devdas, a project that was shelved.

in Tamil Prabhanda and Sanskrit lore. Srisaila had in his lifetime written on the philosophy of Acharya Ramanuja and the mysticism of *Visistadvaita.* Chakravarti and his younger brother Vasudeva, both Sanskrit scholars, took it upon themselves to edit their father's writings and publish it in condensed form. The book was released in Madras in 1974 and was widely reviewed by renowned scholars as well as the media. The edition is recommended at universities for students learning Sanskrit.

The second, his devotion to explore classical dance form. For this, Chakravarti interacted with local artistes, music composers and choreographers, and inspired them to adopt the *kirtans* and *javlis* into assorted dance items for Hema's Bharatanatyam shows. It's interesting how Chakravarti got drawn to these creations. When he discovered that the *nrityas* Hema performed, comprised his daily prayers of the Vishnu *shlokas,* he worked towards adapting them into dance form. Says Hema, 'Every time I got back from an outdoor shoot Appa would surprise me with a new composition for my shows … Andal's *tirupavai* … Thyagraja's *kirtans* … Uthakad's *padams* … I wonder from where he discovered these new music composers and choreographers, but the dance items were always refreshing. After a few days of practise I would have mastered the steps and we would be ready for the show. I enjoyed the challenges and surrendered to my father's better judgement.'

Initially, Hema would perform only pure Bharatanatyam compositions on stage. Gradually as her shows became more popular, the promoters began putting pressure on her to include lighter moments in the concerts. 'All those who wanted access to me and could not, found an easy way out to reach me via these dance shows. Most of them had little interest in dance so after a while the Tamil and Telugu renditions became too heavy going for them. Half way through the show they would shout for Hindi songs, not realizing that most classical art forms are in Sanskrit because they are associated with the temples. The promoters urged Amma to find a solution. It was more out of exasperation that Amma included "*Pag ghungroo bandh* ..." from the *Legend of Meera*. This was some consolation. What the star-struck audience really craved for was a film number, which I was not willing to perform. I took a clear stand that if they wanted "item numbers" they should go to cinema halls,' she remarks resolutely.

It took some time but finally Hema was able to cultivate a definite audience for her shows. It was on the basis of these successful concerts that she was able to, in her later years, design mega ballets under the guidance of ace film and stage choreographer Bhushan Lakhandri. These ballets featured legendary women of substance like Savitri, Durga, Meera and Draupadi. The saint obsessed with Lord Ranganatha was Chakravarti's all-time favourite character. 'Appa was so well-versed with the subject that he always came up with concrete suggestions to improve the script. I valued his inputs and cherished the time spent with him ... ' recalls Hema.

As Hema's popularity grew, Chakravarti found it necessary to open a branch of the Natyavihar Kala Kendra in Bombay as well. 'It is said that I discovered my father very late in life. In our growing-up years, my brothers and I maintained a distance from him. This was partly because he was always busy and also because we feared him and preferred to communicate with him via Amma. In those days, whenever my parents had an argument, I always felt that my mother was right. Today, I feel guilty for being so prejudiced. Because we spent more time with Amma, she had a greater influence on us. As children, Appa was someone who came from the office, read the papers and signed our report cards. But post-retirement he was a transformed man. In the past he was reluctant to accompany me to outdoor locations. But as Amma got more weighed down with my date hassles, Appa willingly came along for my shootings and we spent some wonderful times together on the sets of *Kudrat* and *Mehbooba*. Being with him had a calming effect on me. He had a strong sense of righteousness that did not falter till the end,' she elaborates sentimentally. Hema

Hema Malini with Jeetendra in a still from Dulhan.

was the apple of her father's eye but for Chakravarti there was no compromise on principles even for her. He was affected every time Hema was dragged into controversies.

Scandals and link-ups followed Hema from studio to studio and often led to heartburns. The underlying tension sometimes affected film shootings. An oft-repeated story is when Sanjeev Kumar sent his mother to meet Hema's parents for her hand in marriage and Jaya Chakravarti gracefully declined the proposal on grounds that she was too young to settle down. Not discouraged, Sanjeev requested his colleague and friend Jeetendra, who was shooting a number of films with Hema at the time, to put in a word for him. Jeetendra, it is said, in all earnestness emphasized on the virtues of his friend. 'He is simple, humble and most importantly – single,' Jeetendra is believed to have said. Hema recognized all that and appreciated Sanjeev's feelings for her. She liked him too but not to the extent of wanting to spend her life with him and had the courage to say so.

It is said that Sanjeev Kumar could not handle the rejection and took to drinking heavily. His friends blamed Jeetendra of manipulating Hema's affection but those close to Hema reveal that Jeetendra was completely transparent. It was only when he was sure that Hema was not attracted to Sanjeev that he confessed his adoration for her. The two were shooting for director C.V. Rajendran's *Dulhan* in Bangalore and got to spend a lot of time together. It was apparent to everyone on the sets that Jeetendra was head over heels in love with her. His intentions were noble. He wanted to marry her. Those close to Hema recommended Jeetendra as a prospective suitor. He was handsome, considerate and single. Hema didn't say so openly but appeared to be inclined too. Jeetendra did not waste any time in pursuing her. When the shooting of *Dulhan* drew to a close he summoned his parents to Madras and asked Hema to call her parents there as well.

In the evening the two families met at Hema's bungalow to finalize the alliance, Chakravarti though at home, stayed upstairs refusing to participate in the discussions. Unfortunately, the conversation did not progress because both Hema and Jeetendra were hounded by desperate phone calls from their respective beloveds. Shobha Sippy, then working as an airhostess was a long-time girlfriend of Jeetendra, and Dharmendra everybody knew was crazy about Hema. They urged them to not take any hurried decision. Jeetendra persisted that they should just travel to Tirupati and get married. For a brief moment Hema consented, but then something held her back. Call it fear, caution or just hesitancy to commit, Hema pleaded for some more time to take her decision. Jeetendra was disappointed but he relented. The grapevine was full of stories about what transpired between the two after that. Some blamed Hema for failing to take a firm stand while others blamed Jeetendra for being impatient to take decisions. The real reason for their parting, after all these years remains a mystery but there is no denying that there was a lot of heartbreak. The speculations came to an end when a few months later Jeetendra got married to Shobha Sippy on 31 October 1974.

It was the scandal of the year and the media went to town on the headlines. Producers were grateful that all the negative publicity did not come in the way of the working relationship between Hema and Jeetendra. Except for a brief awkward gap, the pair continued to sign films together beginning with *Jyoti* in 1981, *Hum Tere Aashiq Hain,* and *Mulzim* right up to *Jaan Hatheli Pe* in 1987. Hema was fortunate that none of the turmoil in her personal life ever affected her stardom. She was still the first choice of all producers. On the home front the Chakravartis felt disgraced by the entire episode and a pall of gloom hung over the house. Jaya even began to wonder if in the circumstances wisdom lay in setting aside convention and accepting Dharmendra as the son-in-law. With some trepidation, she broached the subject with her husband. But Chakravarti was appalled at the suggestion. He was not willing to forsake his daughter's future for the temptation of temporary happiness – as he was convinced 'marriage' to Dharmendra would be – and remained obstinate till the end. He believed that the blemish would subside eventually but endorsing the relationship with Dharmendra would only bring doom!

Hema was willing to surrender to any solution provided by the family as long as it guaranteed her sanity. She wanted peace at all cost. 'I will do as you say,' she told her father. Chakravarti sought a practical answer by lining up prospective Iyengar grooms for his daughter. Every Sunday, he invited qualified professionals, engineers and IAS officers for tea at home. 'When it was time I was summoned from my room to join the conversation. Most of these prospective grooms were so nervous in my presence that their tea cups and saucers rattled in their hands,' she recalls with wry amusement today.

A few scattered sentences and Chakravarti had to concede that the suitors could not really live up to his daughter's expectations. She had gone too far ahead for anyone to match her step. 'Perhaps that's the price of success,' says a wistful Hema.

'Unequals don't find entry in a cordoned zone. And the road is too steep to cross alone.' It is a mystery though why no leading industrialist, politician or maestro asked for this exquisite lady's hand or why her family could not find a royal groom for their daughter. And since that was not to be, Hema had to reconcile to finding a beloved from a world she was acquainted with. That Dharmendra was a leading star, shielded her from stigma within the film fraternity. For the time being at least there was relief from the probing media.

Chakravarti was unrelenting and in the meantime years went by. Hema's popularity was unstoppable. As the female superstar she was fetching a price unprecedented. Chakravarti tried his best to balance her rising income but beyond a point, the retired government officer could not cope. Hema's chartered accountant tried his best to find a solution, but the paperwork got more and more complicated. The mounting pressure transformed Chakravarti into an anxious man. Hema recalls her father those days forever bent over files, spectacles on nose, rummaging

In one of her lighter moods with her father, V.S.R. Chakravarti.

through papers. 'In the mornings when I would leave for my shooting, he would call me to sit beside him and understand my tax problems. I would say I don't need to because you are there for me. He would get angry, say it was my money and I should look after it. Appa always said that one must reserve equal time to invest the money we earn, only then can we safeguard our future.

At Hema's birthday party hosted by producer S.N. Jain. Seen here are (from left to right) Dharmendra, Hema Malini, Mrs Akhtar Arif, S.N. Jain and Raaj Kumar.

Unfortunately, I understood the enormity of this very late in life, after he was gone.'

July 1978 was a morbid monsoon for the Chakravartis and ironically, disaster struck in the form of an admirer. A Pakistani fan had been waiting outside Hema's bungalow for over a week for a glimpse of the actress. Every morning he watched her car zoom past the gate but never got an opportunity to meet her. Day after day, he waited from dawn till dusk until Hema returned from work, but her security never allowed him inside the gate.

One morning, fed up of his persistence, the security was slightly harsh on the fan and he did not take to this kindly. At midnight on 20 July after the bungalow lights were turned out, the stranger climbed over the boundary wall into the garden and entered the first floor bedroom, which he presumed was the actress' boudoir. But it was Hema's brother Jagannath's room and the maid was putting his little one to sleep when she saw a strange shadow behind the curtains. She went out to check the door and on finding an intruder, screamed!

Within moments the bungalow was flooded in lights. Chakravarti charged out of his room and flung himself at the stranger. Like a true Hindi film hero he rained fist blows on him. However, the stranger was armed with a knife and used it to scare everyone. Somehow the house servants nabbed him and Chakravarti had the presence of mind to run down and phone the police. When he raced up the staircase again he was panting heavily. By this time Hema, sensing commotion, charged down and was alarmed to find her father gasping. The family rushed him inside the room but it was too late. His head placed on Hema's lap and eyes filled with fear, Chakravarti was fighting for his breath, and before the family knew, he was gone. The doctor arrived soon after and declared it as a diabetic heart attack. The date was 20 July 1978.

For years after that Hema could never talk about her father's demise or perform a similar scene in her films. Deep down she held herself responsible for the tragedy caused by her crazy fan. Today she has matured to view the incident more realistically. 'Few people realize what parents of a popular daughter have to endure. There are too many social and financial pressures and not everyone has the nerves to bear it,' says Hema trifle sadly.

Two years after Chakravarti's death, Hema tied the knot with Dharmendra in 1980. For a while Jaya Chakravarti felt that by going against his wishes, she was betraying her husband's memory. However, Hema's guruma convinced the family that it was an appropriate decision. And odd as it may sound, under the circumstances, the alliance seemed the only option. The repercussions could be dealt with later.

Says Hema, 'As far as I know, I have never intentionally hurt my mother. Except in my choice of marriage partner, perhaps. That was a very tough decision for the entire family to accept. Though today, I wonder if it would have been as painful for them had there been another daughter in the family or had I not been in the public eye … I guess the decision was inevitable. It was not

Hema Malini and Dharmendra got married in a simple Iyengar wedding ceremony on 2 May 1980.

as if he wooed me with roses or took me for moonlight drives. On the contrary, he never paid me any compliments. He praised me behind my back though. Sometimes when I would prod him for his approval, all he would say was, "You are okay and everything is fine." Quite like my mother! It was almost as if I had transferred custody from my mother to my beloved. At times, I feel I was attracted to him because he was so much like my mother, strong and silent,' she muses.

Those were trying times and had Hema and Dharmendra wavered even slightly about their feelings for each other, they may have broken up. But they did not. Torn between love and duty, the couple hung on to a silent commitment. Dharmendra urged Hema to have faith in him and be patient. She trusted his intentions and was willing to endure the brickbats. In those days, when Dharmendra assured Hema that he would come up with a solution, Hema imagined that they would probably settle down in

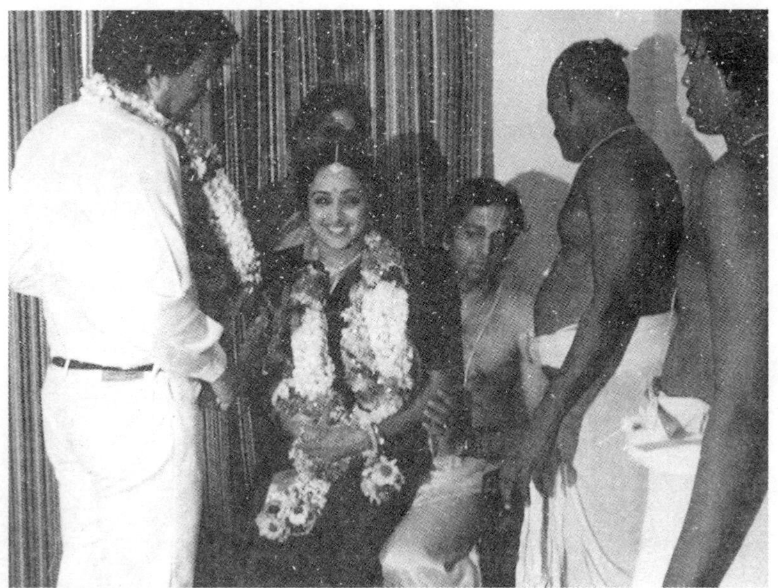

A rare photograph of Hema and Dharmendra's wedding. The marriage was announced a few weeks after they tied the knot.

Bangalore. 'It is my dream city and I fantasized that I could be totally happy there. At that point, I never imagined that we could be living in Bombay. But then, I had never contemplated so many other things like working after marriage and motherhood. I had prior commitments that needed to be honoured. Besides, at no stage did I announce that I was quitting films. It was a wise move since nothing that I have planned has ever worked out.'

The speculations came to an end the day they announced

their marriage. This was some weeks after they officially tied the knot on 2 May 1980, in a quiet ceremony performed as per Iyengar traditions at Hema's bungalow in Juhu and attended by just the family including Dharmendra's late father. The couple sought dignity in silence. Part of the credit for this goes to them and the other part, to their good fortune that they did manage to

Hema and Dharmendra: 'We will always cherish the time we spent together.'

survive the controversies. Perhaps, a similar situation would not have been as volatile in Hollywood. 'But in our society people enjoy discussing other people's personal lives,' shrugs Hema. 'We all have a right to privacy and it should be respected. An outsider has no right to pass moral judgements without knowing the complete story. Even today, when in the course of a serious

Hema and Dharmendra: Days after marriage were blissful.

interview, immature journalists ask questions about my past, I avoid answering them without getting provoked ... When one is in love one wants to share the beautiful experience but I disapprove of lovers shouting confessions from the rooftops. Why must they go public about something so intimate? After all, love brings on certain responsibilities ...

'It's not necessary that everything be discussed threadbare. Not with the press particularly. In my long career, sometimes I did

Hema and Dharmendra after marriage: Certain experiences like marriage are predestined and providential.

not get along with a co-star, sometimes there were problems with a filmmaker, but that did not come in the way of our work. Today, at the slightest disagreement amongst co-stars, shootings are cancelled. Nobody cares for the losses incurred by the producer. You realize this only when you turn a producer yourself. Love is the most precious thing in life, but it has its own place. It cannot come in the way of your work and if it does, it is not love, but indulgence,' she points out emphatically.

Hema believes that certain experiences are meant to be endured. That is destiny. The fact that she was drawn to Dharmendra was predestined. That she should be attracted towards him and none of her other heroes, was providential. That she was willing to risk societal pressures and moral accusations – was the will of God. 'Something like this cannot blossom with just longing … The passion has to ignite from both sides,' she adds.

She strongly resents being referred to as the first lady of second marriages. She does not like the term. 'It is not as if I set out to be the trendsetter. That would be trivializing the feeling and the relationship. There have been so many relationships before and after us but ours was genuine and therefore, it has sustained. I cannot be held responsible for every woman in a similar situation, neither can I be compared with anyone. There are different circumstances in people's lives and I'm not seeking endorsement … It had to happen and I have no regrets. Dharamji has faith in my competence. After all these years, he still looks at me like he did when we first met. He makes me feel special,' she says with a faraway look of happiness.

Historical Moments

Hema believes that films come to actors with a larger message of life. She says that it is her devotion to Lord Krishna and her guru, Ma Indiraji that won her the title role of *Meera*. There is an interesting story about how the idea of *Meera* was conceived. Hema was going through a turbulent phase when Smita, her sister-inlaw-to-be introduced her to their family's guru, Ma Indiraji. Those were days when the media constantly harped about her relationship with Dharmendra. There were instances when he bashed up leading columnists for making derogatory remarks about Hema. He was possessive to the point of obsession but hesitant to make a commitment for obvious reasons. And Hema was suffering ...

One morning as she was leaving for shooting, she received a call from the studio that the shooting was cancelled. 'I held back the information from everybody. For a change my staff was not travelling with me and was to join me directly at the studio. I just got into my car and asked the driver to move on. He had strict instructions from the family to never take me anywhere unescorted. At first, he was reluctant but I insisted and he

Facing Page: *Irrespective of their box office success or failure, some films always remain very special for an artiste. Hema in a still from* Ramkali.

relented. When we drove closer to Chembur, I told him to drive me to Poona. He was shocked but did not dare to oppose me. I was taken aback by my own daring but something was leading me there . . .'

In Poona, Hema drove directly to Ma's ashram. The devotees were surprised to see her since there was no intimation about her visit. They would not let her in until they had spoken to Ma on the intercom to ask if she was expecting the actress. Ma asked them to lead her inside. 'When I entered her room, she was in a discourse with her disciples. She smiled and motioned me to sit beside her. I participated in the discourse and when it ended, continued to hang around her. I cannot remember what we talked about but I spent that entire day with her. We had lunch together and later I rested in the ashram. She asked me no questions and I felt healed just being in her presence,' Hema reveals a lesser-known fact of her life.

By this time Hema's family had learnt that her shooting was cancelled and were worried about her whereabouts. They had called all friends and relatives whom she could have visited but she was nowhere to be found. In panic they had also called Dharmendra but even he did not know where she was. Finally, it was Jaya Chakravarti who thought of contacting Ma Indiraji at her Poona ashram. Ma told Jaya not to worry about her daughter because she was safe with her and would be spending the night with her at the ashram, and return the following day. 'She also added that when I came home nobody should ask me any questions, and for a change, they did not,' Hema recalls the feeling of liberation with a smile.

After this episode it became a pattern with Hema to seek out Ma Indiraji every time she was distressed. 'Strangely, I was not drawn to her for her spirituality. That understanding came much later. At that point all that mattered to me was that her presence made me feel peaceful,' she relates. Quietly and unobtrusively Ma led Hema on to the path of spirituality. 'She would talk to me about life and karma . . . about the courageous tales of many

Seeking blessing from her guruma, Ma Indiraji: Quietly and unobtrusively Ma led Hema on to the path of spirituality.

mythological characters ... their faith and sacrifice ... She was particularly fond of Meera. "You must play Meera in your film some day," she would always tell me,' says Hema.

One evening when Hema returned from her visit to the ashram, filmmaker Premji was waiting for her at home. Premji had been keen to make a film with Hema for many years but nothing had worked out. He had a couple of scripts but Hema was not drawn to any. 'If you would be interested in making a film on Meera I would love to play the part,' she told Premji.

The very next day Premji signed up Gulzar to write and direct the film. But problems hounded *Meera* from the day of the mahurat. First, Lata Mangeshkar opted out of the project because she had recently cut an album on Meera bhajans and did not want to repeat herself. Then, music directors Laxmikant and Pyarelal backed out because they did not want to work without Lata. Undeterred, Gulzar went and signed Pt Ravi Shankar for the compositions and Vani Jairam for the playback. But Hema was not convinced. Lata Mangeshkar had sung all her songs beginning with *Sapno Ka Saudagar* and she felt that her performance would not be the same without Lata's ethereal playback. She personally requested Lata to sing for the film but the nightingale held on to her own. 'I must admit that I'm psychologically dependent on Lata Mangeshkar's voice. If my filmmakers have etched various characters I have played, Lataji has added to these roles with her voice. I cannot imagine any of my performance without her melodious songs,' she adds.

Bhanu Athaiya designed the costumes for *Meera*. Hema reveals that it was a humbling experience to watch her devotion to her job. She would spend hours checking out the fabric and the drape of every costume. For an outsider, the costumes may seem a clear division between the princess and the saint but watching her work from close quarters, Hema reveals that Bhanu had a special knack for matching the character's varied moods and phases with relevant hues and fabrics. There were times she would argue endlessly with the director for want of just a slightly varied shade of beige sari. 'At that time all of us thought she was too fussy, but today I understand that Bhanuji had worked out an entire journey of the character through these slightly varied shades,' recalls Hema. 'Beginning with the blushing bride in radiant hues, I move on to sober shades, until I don the saffron robe when leaving the palace. Gradually, the saffron saris change to pale yellow, fawn and beige when I finally surrender to the Lord. Unlike stars of today, we could not bully our dress-designers into giving us what we felt suited us better. Even the size and the length of the tulsi mala I wore in the film was determined by the designer. That is why I say that the characters I portrayed belonged as much to my directors as to my designers.'

The shooting of the film began soon after but Premji had to still confirm a hero. No leading actor was willing to play King Rana, perceived as a weak man in literature. Finally, Vinod Khanna, who owed his break in films to Gulzar's *Mere Apne,* agreed. There was more: because of the subject and the casting, the film turned grossly over-budget and producer Premji felt he would not be able to afford Hema Malini's astronomical price. He could not ask her to reduce her remuneration, so he worked out a settlement wherein he paid Hema on a daily basis. Every evening, Premji handed an envelope to the actress, which she placed inside her cupboard unopened. 'I had agreed to do the film for my love for Lord Krishna and for my guruma. Whatever I got I took it as a blessing from them and have not used that money to this day,' she discloses.

Even today, Hema believes that she got the opportunity to play Meera as a result of Ma's blessings. 'It's strange the kind of effect some people have on your life. Guruma reminded me of a dense tree that shelters travellers. I had to merely see her face or hear her voice and my biggest anxieties would subside automatically. That's the power of healing,' she elaborates.

Meera, released in 1979, did not fare well at the box office. Writer-director Gulzar said it was because the film told more about the woman than the saint and the audience could not relate

Meera: *A dream role Hema cherishes and feels proud of.*

to that. Neither producer Premji nor Hema had any regrets about the dismal fate of the film. Hema remembers Gulzar telling her that it would be a film she would be proud to watch with her children and grandchildren. *Meera* remains Hema's all-time favourite, a film she is immensely proud of to this date. 'My favourite scenes in the film are all those moments where I'm in argument with my guru. The content of the conversation and the social message imparted via the dialogues is very powerful. But the most dramatic shot comes in the climax when Meera, tied in chains (resembling Jesus Christ), is presented before the court. As she walks into the room, her larger-than-life shadow casts over the guru and he feels frightened. It was a highly cinematic shot dramatically projected by the director,' she stresses. The film proved a milestone in Hema's career. It was the beginning of her pairing with Vinod Khanna, and the end with Shammi Kapoor who earlier played her hero in Ramesh Sippy's *Andaaz*. In *Meera* Shammi Kapoor played Hema's father, King Rathod.

Raj Kapoor once said that actors lend their destiny to a film and slowly, the film becomes a part of their destiny. In fact the role comes their way because it is going to transform their fortunes.

Kamaal Amrohi considered Hema for *Razia Sultan* even though she was not well versed in Urdu, a basic requirement for the character. But Hema had all the other personality traits. She had a regal bearing and superstar stature essential to make a heroine-oriented project feasible. There is another reason why Amrohi cast Hema. He was researching in Turkistan Archives where he came across a photograph of Razia that had a striking resemblance to Hema Malini. That was the time Amrohi decided on casting her as the Turkish princess.

When he finally approached Hema for the role, he is supposed to have told her that if she trusted him he would give her a performance of a lifetime. She trusted him wholeheartedly and signed the project. She walked on hot sands, rode elephants and horses, enacted sword fights and wore uncomfortable crowns

A performance of a lifetime: On the sets of Razia Sultan *with director Kamaal Amrohi and Dharmendra.*

and costumes that left blemishes. Learning Urdu dialogues was a tough proposition and the determined filmmaker hired a special teacher to supervise her diction constantly. Hema with her characteristic candour admits, 'I knew it was going to be a difficult role and was prepared for the hard work. I had seen *Pakeezah* and loved it. Every frame of the film is like a painting and the characters are absolutely extraordinary.'

It was the most expensive film made during that time, about a Turkish Emperor Altamash who chose his daughter over his sons as his heir and successor. It dwelt on a queen's love for her Assyrian slave, Yaqut. Five renowned lyricists came together for the first time to offer their best poetry – Kaifi Azmi, Kamaal Amrohi, Jaan Nisar Akhtar, Nida Fazli and Kaif Bhopali. Lata Mangeshkar rendered one of her best songs '*Ai dile naadan …* ' picturized on a stunningly stately Razia – Hema in the hot sands of Rajasthan.

There were lavish sets put up at the newly launched Kamalistan Studio in Mahakali Caves, Andheri and foreign technicians were hired. It is said that Amrohi purchased a pot full of pearls to construct the magnificent Motimahal set. Camels and horses were brought from Rajasthan and special tailors and embroiderers invited from Turkey to lend an authenticity to the costumes. But the best story was happening on the personal front, which nobody knew at that time. Towards the final schedule of *Razia Sultan,* Hema Malini conceived her firstborn, Esha.

There was a brief period during 1978-79 when Hema was shooting for *Meera* and *Razia Sultan* simultaneously. *Meera* in the mornings because Gulzar is an early riser and *Razia Sultan* in the evenings because of the elaborate lighting. 'The characters belonged to two different eras but in a strange way were very similar. If Razia was the empress, Meera was the pauper princess. Adjusting to both the roles was not difficult because the directors were well prepared and guided me at every step. Sometimes I feel that actors make too much fuss about preparing for a role. I can't understand how certain artistes live with the same character for four and five years … I find it impractical. After all, it is just a film and life has to move on … *Razia Sultan* was an intriguing film but it took seven years to complete and hence lost a part of its magic,' she analyses pragmatically.

In the meanwhile, the little drop of life within Hema was growing and the only person privy to the explosive secret was Dharmendra. Hema did not want anyone to know her secret and so did not reveal it to anybody. 'I did not want anyone cross-examining me or passing judgements and this included my family. So for the first time in my life I kept a secret even from my mother. I avoided confiding even in my aunts who I was close to, for fear that they might confess it to Amma. I was fortunate that I was in good health and did not suffer the usual morning sickness associated with early pregnancies. Every morning, I left for shooting at my regular time and for a long time nobody was even slightly suspicious or thought anything amiss,' she chuckles bemusedly.

But gradually the 'bump' started showing. Besides, Hema was forever hungry on the sets and kept asking for sweets. 'I'm sure the production units got curious but nobody questioned me directly and I preferred not to explain. Soon, Amma became doubtful and confronted me. I could not lie to her and confessed the truth. She was anxious and suggested we inform my producers. But I was still not willing to do so. I delayed breaking the news for as long as six months and in the process had to endure many difficult horse-riding and dance sequences,' she relates. The film fraternity was abuzz with rumours though. Her colleagues discussed it in whispers on the sets but none had the courage to make a public statement. Her cameramen suspected but had no complaints for there was an added glow to her face and she looked radiant. The media too speculated but none dared to question her directly. Her progressing pregnancy can be noticed in the long shots of films like *Rajput* and *Satte Pe Satta* shot during her last months. 'My directors were careful to shoot me only in close-ups and I was fortunate I had not swollen up. When Raj Sippy approached me for *Satte Pe Satta,* I had to tell him the truth. He did not mind working with me because he felt the extra weight went well with the character. The seven heroes including Amitabh Bachchan were protective of me on the sets,' she reminisces.

In between their hectic schedules, Dharmendra and Hema Malini took out free time to go for a short vacation to London. 'On this trip I was only interested in shopping at Mothercare. I would stop at all the children's counters and Dharamji would feel shy. He always made some excuse and sauntered away but it did not deter me. We had initially planned to have my delivery abroad, but later, both Dharamji and I felt that it would not be practical without the family support,' says Hema.

Stories about Hema's pregnancy were as dramatic as her marriage and courtship. It is said that Dharmendra booked her in several hospitals simultaneously to deliberately mislead the media. He blocked all the rooms of a private nursing home in the suburbs because he did not want any outsiders invading the premises.

Hema has vivid memories of those days. After shooting two and three shifts a day for years, this was the first time she was spending free time at home. For the first few weeks she enjoyed the peace but after a while, the idleness turned her restless. She felt the need to use her time constructively and her mother suggested that she try her hand at painting. Jaya Chakravarti had produced her best paintings when she was pregnant and Hema followed in her mother's footsteps. 'I was working till the end of the eighth month and was homebound only in the ninth month. During this time my father-in-law presented me with a beautiful picture of Lord Krishna. I was so fascinated with the visual that I was driven to painting the picture on canvas.'

As the 'expected date of delivery' drew closer, her doctor got panicky because Hema showed no signs of going into labour. One night Dharmendra was visiting her and had to leave for a preview of a film and that's when Hema developed cramps and he rushed her to the hospital. 'I was taken in my brother's car to avoid attention. The following hours were a nightmare but I felt safe holding on to Dharamji's hand who was all the time present in the labour room. Finally, Esha arrived by dawn. It was the second of November in the winter of 1981,' Hema's eyes light up as maternal memories come flooding in. For a while nobody would tell me that it was a girl … they thought I would be disappointed. But when I held my little baby in my arms, I knew that I would not exchange her for any son in the world,' smiles Hema. According to the couple's plan, Dharmendra kept Esha's birth a secret for five days.

Once the news became public there were predictable assumptions and conclusions but it was not as if there were no moments of relief. There were innumerable occasions when Hema's life sparkled with the newfound joy of motherhood. Away from the prying media and acrimonious reactions, Hema relished her real role of a mother. She continued to live in the sprawling bungalow on 12th Road, Juhu Vile Parle Development Scheme and Dharmendra in his own home. But the two bungalows were just a street away, and Dharmendra spent as much time with his new family as possible. Hema sees the fact that she never bore a son as a message from God. 'He cannot, after all, grant me everything. He granted me the man I loved and that by itself was a miracle. To ask for more favours from him would be avaricious ... Esha's face resembles the image I painted of the Lord Krishna. In fact, I named her Esha because it means divine beloved. It's a Sanskrit word suggested by my guru and very sacred to all of us,' she smiles.

In show business, chemistry alters after marriage and it happened with Hema and Dharmendra as well. While in the past, even films where they made just a special appearance like *Barood* and *Swami* were big hits, now the best of banners could not revive their magic. Several filmmakers tried, but the box office turned down all efforts. And perhaps it was best this way. The new relationship had brought with it inevitable stress and strain in Dharmendra's 'regular' home. New equations had to be established, and until that happened, it was prudent for the pair to not work together for some time. The last film in which they were paired together was Kamaal Amrohi's *Razia Sultan*, which released in 1983.

Four years passed by and to a large extent the brewing tensions settled down. Dharmendra was still active as a hero and his elder son Sunny Deol was a star to reckon with. Hema was pregnant for the second time. And once again she hoped for a son but only so that it completed the family. Today though, she cannot imagine her life without her daughters. 'No experience can substitute the joy of watching your daughters grow ... In their dreams, I have somewhere sought my lost childhood ... ' she says as her eyes moisten just slightly.

She says, as a father, Dharmendra is firm but indulgent. In the earlier days he was more worried about their school report cards. 'I don't know what kind of a student he made, but he was very keen that the girls fared well in academics. "Are they scoring good marks?" he would always ask me. Today, he worries about their welfare – always emphasizing that they should be well-behaved and disciplined. Esha and Ahana share a good equation with him. They are not scared of him unless of course they have been naughty. Both know that they can get anything out of him. When they want his attention, they will try every trick in the book. He spoils them silly but they are responsible enough to not betray his faith,' she states with maternal pride.

Hema feels that she has a lot for which to thank god for. Blessed with a loving family, good health and a flourishing art, she could not ask for more. 'Certain deprivations persist in day-to-day life but priorities in life alter with time,' she summarizes. As long as both the girls were in primary school, Hema personally went to drop her daughters to school everyday. 'Their timing was eight in the morning. I'd wait in my car till I saw them walk to the building. After that I would come home, do my make-up and leave for shooting. I had told my producers that I will only report for work after packing off my children to school and everyone co-operated. I stopped dropping the girls at school only after they went into the secondary section and that too because they were embarrassed. They did not want me chaperoning them. Till they completed their final year in school, no matter where I was shooting, I was always present for their PTA meetings and annual functions …

'These moments were special because both of them always participated in dance activities. And as a mother it was enlightening for me to watch them in unfamiliar surroundings. Parents take children for granted but they are forever surprising us. They come up with the most fascinating observations. When Ahana was a child and visited me on the sets, she was curious why so many people crowded around me. Then one day out of the blue she asked me, "Do they follow you because you are a queen … ?" I was so amused. It is always difficult to read what goes on in a child's mind. I am not an over-anxious mother as long as both of them are well-behaved and understand their responsibilities. I don't have unrealistic expectations from anybody and that includes my children. I would like it if both of them pursue some form of art along with their personal choice of careers. This can only enrich them. Art is demanding, I agree, and takes away their free time, but eventually the exercise will prove fruitful. A time will come when friends, family and time will wither away and only art will nourish them. I grudged it when I was forced to learn dance in childhood. Today, I am grateful to my mother for not giving in to my whims and being persistent. Dance has enriched me. It's because of my formal training in classical dance that I was also able to sustain a position in my film career,' she admits with endearing humility.

Moods and Moments

Hema divides dance into three definite phases in her life. The first, when she performed as a little girl. 'After the initial nervousness when I had become accustomed to the darkness in the auditorium, I felt like a fairy walking over the clouds … It was almost as if the audience did not exist.' The third, when she launched her dance ballets, 'When I stepped on to the stage in my costume, I got transformed into the character and lived with her long after the lights went out.' And in between these two phases is the long period when she performed various numbers for her films. Dancing in films, she clarifies, is more about timing your steps than about feelings or melody, 'It's difficult to infuse emotion when the shooting of an *antara* or a *mukhda* stretches over a few days. In the given circumstances, actors learn to switch on and off … '

Over her three-decade long film career, Hema Malini got opportunities to dance on songs depicting every mood and moment in Hindi films. If in *Charas* she did a Cleopatra dance, then in *Dus Numbri*, she was a bartender. In *Jaaneman* she did a *mujra,* and in *Swami,* a *nautanki.* In *Meera,* she swayed with a

Facing Page: *As a trained classical dancer, Hema found it a little embarrassing to do the vigorous movements given by the dance directors. Hema in a still from* Do Thug.

Hema cherishes her moments of abhinaya *and* nritya.

tanpura inside a temple and in *Alibaba Aur 40 Chor*, for the first time, she did an Arabic belly dance. In *The Burning Train*, Parveen Babi and she compete between eastern and western tradition. In *Jyoti*, she danced the *dandiya raas* with a child star. She recalls how her steps during the waltz dancing with Raaj Kumar in *Sharara* had to be perfectly timed, and she had to depict an abandon as a crooner in *Naseeb*.

Hema opines that it is tough to perform regular dance if your body is trained for a classical form, 'The first time I was exposed to a different dance form was when I did the item number for my two South films – *Pandav Vanvas* (Telegu) and *Idu Satyam* (Tamil). Both these numbers had me centre stage along with group dancers. In Hindi films, the first dance was for *Sapno Ka Saudagar*. All memories related to dance in this film are associated with extreme body ache.' Hema just could not adjust to the energetic movements demonstrated by Hindi films' ace choreographer, Hiralal Master. He would make her go through extensive rehearsals for days at a stretch. His vigorous movements repulsed Hema and no matter how loudly he yelled at her, she just could not get herself to heave her bosom or copy his overtly suggestive facial expressions, like biting of the lower lip. 'When it was time for the "take", I would enact the movements in a manner that came naturally to me and during close-ups, rather than ape the dance master's expressions that suited him, I would merely smile ...' laughs Hema.

As a child, her dance teacher had taught her that while on stage, if ever she missed a beat or forgot her step, she must take a steady position and smile ... And that is exactly what Hema did before the camera. Because she had a million-dollar smile, the cinematographer would be delighted with the shot. Not the choreographer though. Hiralal Master acknowledged her talent but was nonplussed at a newcomer who was disobeying his instructions. This continued through the shooting of '*Naadan ki dosti jee ka jalana, jane na balam ...*' in *Sapno Ka Saudagar.* Frustrated and exhausted, Hiralal Master finally surrendered to Hema's inhibitions.

Over the years, Hiralal and other dance directors perceived wisdom in choreographing movements that suited Hema Malini's graceful personality rather than adapt her to their stereotypical

Hema's graceful dance movements coupled with this smile would make her come alive on screen. In a still from Tere Mere Sapne.

steps. The solutions worked both ways. Hema was more comfortable and even the audience preferred her in more conservative dances. Says Hema, 'This would not have happened had I succumbed to their initial pressures. Hiralalji understood that I was not being disrespectful. I was genuinely unable to perform the provocative steps. It was a case of cultural differences.'

For the shooting of *Waaris*, Hema had to swing to a rock 'n' roll number with two of film industry's best dancers, Jeetendra and Mehmood. It was a crazy dance number where the heroes were dressed in shorts and freaking out. Hema was given a hideous skirt and blouse, put together by a local tailor in Madras. Hema recalls this was her first group dance and it was difficult to synchronize her steps with the other actors. 'Mehmoodji and Jeetuji being experienced actors, had no problems with the illogical situation of the song ... But still being a newcomer, I was outraged by the acrobatics. I kept grumbling and complaining on the sets till Mehmoodji pulled me aside and explained to me that in cinema there was no logic and as a professional I had to be prepared to deliver the most absurd scenes without questioning ...'

In the same film, Hema had another dance in which she is possessed by a goddess. Hiralal Master who by now had made truce with Hema, compensated for his earlier lapses with some semi-classical movements. 'What I remember about this shooting clearly is the *mukhda* where I had to count one, two, three, four, fall on the floor and then rise. It had to be done very rapidly, and needed rigorous rehearsals. To an extent that I was muttering one ... two ... three ... four ... even in my sleep,' she gurgles with laughter.

In 1969, the song '*Nas nas mein agan tute hain badan ...*' from *Jahan Pyar Mile* was Hema's first dream sequence. She was embarrassed by the explicit lyrics and also the equally explicit movements demonstrated to her. As always, she went through the rehearsals quietly but when it was time for the 'take' she performed the movements her way. The director had instructed the costume designer to provide her a white sari to enhance her sensuousness but Hema made sure that a skin lining was attached to it all over. This was something she followed all through her career. 'They wanted me to wear a short sari reaching above my knees but I felt it looked ridiculous and increased the length of the costume without consulting anyone. I was aware that the dance would involve all kinds of movements ... I did not want to be embarrassed on the sets in front of everyone,' she relates how she changed the rules in her silent way.

It was an accepted practice for lead stars in the 1970s to rehearse with chorus dancers. One out of this large group would substitute as the hero/heroine and the star would learn the steps. 'How I hated the exercise. I hated the idea of a sweaty assistant holding me ... Not that anybody ever overstepped the limits of decency but the entire process was too intimate for comfort. The worst was when the dance master made you practise intricate movements for days at a stretch and then on the day of the actual shooting change the steps completely. All of them invariably did that and it was frustrating to start learning new movements all over again. But nobody complained because the choreographer was the king then.'

Hema worked with ace choreographer P.L. Raj, popularly referred to as Raj Master, for the first time in *Abhinetri* in 1970. She played a classical dancer in the film, married to a scientist who wants his wife to give up her passion for dance. 'Raj Master gave me semi-classical dance steps that suited the character and went well with my personality. I have worn authentic costumes of Bharatanatyam, Kathak and Manipuri dance forms appropriate for the role.' Her costumes for the film were designed by Oscar awardee, Bhanu Athaiya. Hema says one cannot fault Bhanu's colour combinations or choice of fabric. 'She was responsible for my glamorization on screen. The chiffon saris edged with delicate embroidery and sleeveless blouses were all her contribution. Also the big flower tucked in my hair and the sari tucked at the waist. Over the years we did several films together and those were all learning experiences in aesthetics because Bhanu is a master of her craft,' she acknowledges gratefully.

In the same year, jubilee hit *Johnny Mera Naam* featured two of Hema's favourite dances, '*Babul pyaaré ...* ' and '*Chup chup Meera roye ...* '. Interestingly, both were shot around the same time and depicting a tragic mood, the dances, says Hema, reflected her real state of mind at that time. Her personal life was embroiled in tension due to her attraction to Dharmendra. A passive recipient of familial bonds that sometimes strangle without realizing that the victim is choking, Hema had no private space to break down. She could not have an outburst at home and she could not throw a tantrum on the sets, so unknowingly she found release in her emotional scenes. 'There were moments when real tears mingled with glycerine but fortunately nobody could tell except perhaps the camera,' she discloses.

In *Sharafat,* Hema played a prostitute and needed to portray a provocative dance, '*Raja jaani …*' 'I was terribly uncomfortable shooting for this dance and infuriated the director by shying away from the seductive expressions expected of me. My reluctance did not come in the way of the song's popularity later. It had coins raining in theatres but I was far from flattered. In fact, I was repulsed. In the same film, however, I had another equally popular number "*Sharafat chod di maine …*" where the dancer is defeated by her dreams and expresses her feelings through this dance. It called for soft expressions and a sombre mood, and so I was more at ease in shooting for this song.'

Coincidentally, both these songs inspired film titles in later years and Hema starred in both of them. Most films released during the 1970s were formula entertainers and portrayed acrobatic dance numbers. In *Tum Haseen Main Jawan* she was dressed in a shimmering costume and donned a blue wig. 'Dharamji and I had to do a western dance during which I had to climb on to his back. I was quite overweight in those days but chivalrous as he is, he never complained. Today I feel bad about it.'

Hema adds that like all heroines in Hindi films, she had to suffer a number of rain dances. '*Rama rama gajab hui gavare ...*' in 1971 for *Naya Zamana* was her first. The song was included to provide relief in the film that was otherwise too serious. This time again, the costume designer was warned to dress her in a white sari, which Hema changed to yellow worn with a lining. 'My costume designers often got into trouble with the directors because I was obstinate but nobody ever said anything to me and I got used to having my way,' she smiles triumphantly.

In *Paraya Dhan* where Hema played a schoolgirl living in Himachal Pradesh, she had to dance around in the field holding a stick. 'It was not as simple as it looked because the stick had to be

Balancing the stick wasn't easy: Hema Malini with Rakesh Roshan in Paraya Dhan.

balanced without it becoming obtrusive. We don't realize but there is a synchronicity between action and choreography. The reason why everyone says I'm good with action is because I'm a trained dancer. Both call for infinite grace and precise timing and even today, when I watch this song I feel satisfied with my abandon. It is quite refreshing!'

Hema in a still from Raja Jaani.

Hema's first on-screen snake dance from the film Babul Ki Galiyaan.

Vijay Anand cast Hema Malini in *Tere Mere Sapne* because he wanted a dancer for the role. In the film she played an oppressed actress and true to Vijay Anand's reputation, he gave her a spectacular dance, '*Ta thai taka thai* … '. It was a very beautifully shot song and very well choreographed, 'I was given very delicate hand and foot movements. I would say that after "*Piya tose naina lage* … " in *Guide*, this was Goldie saab's best classical dance and I thoroughly enjoyed shooting it.'

Hema learnt that working in Hindi films was all about courting new challenges. *Babul Ki Galiyaan* offered Hema her first snake dance – another must for a leading lady in mainstream cinema. Choreographed by Sohanlal Master, Hiralal's brother, it included a lot of aggressive movements, but gradually Hema was learning to drop her inhibitions.

'*Shanno naam uska* … ' in *Raja Jaani* was Hema's first street dance. It was shot on the roads of Bombay city amidst a 'live' audience. Hema says it was not easy to perform before so many people, particularly since she was expected to bring on seductive expressions, but she somehow managed. She reveals that *Raja Jaani* was a significant film in resolving her conflict between the classical and the film dancer. 'Until this film the classical performer in me ruled over the film dancer. It was during this film that I realized that I couldn't journey through my film career carrying the baggage of my classical training. So for the first time, I let the actress inside me take over the dancer. It was a new beginning,' she relates.

In *Raja Jaani* for the first time Hema worked with another skilful and able costume designer, Leena Daru. Hema is full of praise for Leena's versatility. 'She was so well versed with patterns and cuts that I could entirely depend on her sartorial expertise. They were a different generation altogether. Though all of them were very friendly with stars we could never override their creative judgement. Their loyalty was to the character so if the role demanded from me to look poor, like the tangewali in *Sholay,* I was draped in thick cotton ghagras. In *Kranti,* Leenaji dabbled my costumes in oil for the worn-out effect,' she says shaking her head.

In *Jugnu,* for the dance '*Meri payaliya geet tere gaaye ...* ' Hema performed a regular stage dance number involving three costume changes – the Rajasthani, the Santhali and the Maharashtrian. 'The nine-yard *navvari* was the best of the lot, it is indeed sad that I never got the opportunity to perform a complete *lavani* dance all through my career.'

When she had to shoot for her first cabaret dance in Raj Khosla's *Shareef Badmash,* the director gave specific instructions for her to wear a revealing costume. Dress designer Mani Rabbadi followed her brief but during the dress trial, Hema stubbornly added length and breadth to the existing costume. On the day of the shooting Hema arrived on the sets attired in a full-sleeved gown. Khosla was appalled by this out-of-character costume but since it was getting late for the shot, he decided not to make a fuss. It was a striptease number that required Hema to take off one piece of clothing with each *mukhda,* which she did with great elan, but at the end of the song still managed to remain fully covered. 'What I had projected was nowhere close to the director's original concept. He was so furious with me that he never signed me again!' laughs Hema.

In the film *Haath Ki Safai,* Hema had a dance sequence where she posed as a club dancer. Those days Hema was shooting triple shifts, so the song '*Tu kya jaane bewafa* ...' had to be shot during night shifts. Hema arrived dressed in a low-back gown and shoulder-length hair in a straight cut like the *Seeta Aur Geeta* get-up. The costume had little scope for skin show but then that was not expected of Hema. 'It is not necessary that we associate sensuality with exposure. I wore a halter dress, which I thought was sufficiently revealing. The song is memorable for me because this was my first experience of dancing, holding a mike.' In the same film she had a hilarious dance with Randhir Kapoor performed as a spoof on Sarat Chandra's *Devdas.* She played Chandramukhi while Randhir played Devdas. The song '*Peene waalon ko peene ka bahana chahiye* ... ' was rendered by Kishore Kumar and Hema had to record a few lines '*Devdas mitwa gao, Chandramukhi ke paas aao* ... ' in her own voice.

She has fond memories of '*Ye toh time time ki baat hai* ... ', the party song in *Kasauti* because it was anecdotal and hilarious. Hema wore red pants with a tall black hat and danced with a long stick. 'The song was choreographed by Saloni, a ballet dancer who later taught my children dancing. It's always interesting to work with choreographers from outside the film world. They always add nuances that are refreshing. During this dance I learnt that the trick of performing with a prop is to make it as inconspicuous as possible,' she admits.

In *Patthar Aur Payal*, Hema is abducted by the dacoits and forced to entertain them. The plot was repeated later in several films.

'I have fond memories of the *Dharmatma* dance sequence shot in Afghanistan. It would have been nicer had dance director P.L. Raj included some local steps rather than the same *masala* number. But despite all the shortcomings, the film was a big hit and the songs greatly appreciated,' reflects Hema.

'Jab tak hai jaan ...' : *The song that inspired many similar song situations. Hema in a still from* Sholay.

Hema Malini rates her classical number '*Navroop se rachna rachi jab nar ki, satyam shivam sundaram ...*' in *Mrig Trishna,* released in 1975, as her best dance performance on screen. How the song came to be shot is a story by itself. Producer Nahata was waiting for Hema in Jodhpur with a ready unit but Hema was stuck in combination dates with Ramesh Sippy for *Sholay* in Bangalore. Sippy was reluctant to release Hema even for a few days because his film had run exorbitantly over-budget and got delayed. After a lot of pleading, Sippy relented on condition that Hema would be back in Bangalore on the third day. Hema agreed.

She arrived in Jodhpur late evening and the song was shot over two nights (8 p.m. to 6 a.m. shifts) in the Jodhpur palace. On the third day, a content Hema drove directly from the location to the airport as promised to Sippy. The *Mrig Trishna* dance sequence is an experience she can never forget. 'The lilting music was composed by the renowned Kathak master Shambhu Sen and choreographed by debutante Saroj Khan … There was a magic to the composition because Shambhu Sen as a dancer, understood the beats and intrinsically provided the pauses in his composition,' says Hema and she considers it amongst the supreme dances of Hindi cinema and recommends it to be preserved in the archives as a study in classical choreography. 'Not only are the movements extraordinary, but even the lyrics are rich in meaning and soothing. The dance is symbolic of all the rules of *Natyashastra.* In movement, rhythm, expression and ambience, it is almost perfect.'

In 1975, Hema performed a dance which was to inspire many similar song situations during the decade. '*Jab tak hai jaan* ... ' in *Sholay* proved the most popular track of its time. 'I had to dance on an uneven slope. My feet were bruised with corns and took weeks to heal. After every "take", I would run to wear my *mojris* and remove them a minute before the camera rolled.' The song was picturized in the blistering heat of May in Bangalore because director Ramesh Sippy wanted that effect. Halfway through the song the henchmen throw a bottle on the rocks. Though mock glass was used for most of the shooting for the close-up shots, Hema needed to walk close to the glass pieces. Some of the splinters pierced her heel but she completed the shot without so much as flinching.

Some films turned out to be hits only because the songs became popular '*Prem ka rog bada bura* … ' in *Dus Numbri* was one of them. She played a bar dancer in the song sequence. 'I wore a Goan costume for the number and the choreography matched the requirement of the song,' she declares happily.

All the dances in *Mehbooba* were shot in the Mysore Palace. Hema was satisfied with her attire in the film and also the classical steps she got to perform. She credits Kathak component Gopi Krishna for her intricate expressions during the dance '*Mein mujra karungi* … '. Says Hema nostalgically, 'It's not easy to portray minute, fragile expressions unless somebody is constantly guiding you. Gopiji was a master of expressions. By a mere twitch of an eyebrow he could portray a variety of emotions. It was a pleasure to watch him dance. *Mehbooba* did good business because of its extraordinary music.'

Dream Girl was India's first film to be shot in Disneyland. Obtaining permission to shoot there was almost impossible but somehow the film crew managed to have their way. The song '*Bacchon yeh dekho Disneyland hai …* ' was not recorded during the time of the shooting but since they would not have been able to return to Disneyland again, the director salvaged it by making Hema lip-sync and shoot her from long shots.

Every time Hema felt she was turning complacent, a challenge would come her way to excel herself. In 1977, Gulzar offered her *Kinara*, a film about a dancer who loses her eyesight in an accident. The film delved on a dancer's struggle to conquer her fears and makes her comeback. For the climax where the blind dancer makes her comeback, the director wanted a tension-filled situation where the audience is privy to her handicap. Gulzar was certain that he wanted a prop in the choreography but he was unclear of what it should be. The choreographer and he toyed with many ideas like a sword or a drum but it was not working out. It was Hema's suggestion to use a sharp-edged steel *thali*. The item is a part of the Kuchipudi dance and something Hema was familiar with. Gulzar was convinced and so was the choreographer. That the classical item suited the situation in the film was an added opportunity for Hema to display her skill as a dancer. 'This was perhaps the first time a Kuchipudi item was experimented in mainstream films and I compliment Gulzar saab for his vision. Performing under Gopiji was of course always a treat. Somehow he had a knack of enacting the most versatile expressions to the simplest of words. This is apparent in all V. Shantaram dances, be it *Navrang* or *Sehra*. It was always challenging for me to dance with him and in the coming years with his younger brother Madhavji … '

Hema with choreographer Gopi Krishna. Gopiji could portray minute and very fragile expressions. It was always a pleasure for Hema to work with Gopiji.

Compared to all the rain sequences she had done so far, Manoj Kumar's *Kranti* was by far the most difficult. She had to suffer a harrowing rain song where she rolled on a hard floor, her hands tied back with a rope. '*Zindagi ki na tute ladi ...* ' became a controversial subject for the media only because journalists could not digest Hema in a drenched-to-skin costume. Hema refused to rise to the bait. She was more concerned about completing the shooting without injuring her back. 'The process of rolling on the wooden floor was very painful and I dreaded hurting myself. However, when I saw the film I forgot all my misgivings. Cinema is about team spirit. When the end product is satisfactory all the hardships are forgotten. That's the joy of a creative process and experience,' she concludes.

For the shooting of this song in Naseeb *Hema arrived dressed in a black gown looking ravishing.*

In *Naseeb* Hema once more played a club dancer and for the title song '*Mere naseeb mein tu hai ké nahi* … ' arrived dressed in a fully covered black gown not expected of the character. This time again the director could not complain because Hema looked ravishing in a fur stole stylishly flung around her neck matched with a glamorous fringed hairstyle.

For *Lekin,* Hema performed a Kathak dance composed by renowned choreographer Roshan Wajifdar. It involved intricate steps and Gulzar was surprised that Hema could pick up the most difficult movements very easily. Hema cherishes her *mujra 'Joothe naina* … ' rendered by Asha Bhonsle and Satyasheel Deshpande, particularly the composition interspersed with the tabla beats.

Unlike most films that just add an item number, there was a specific reason for this dance in the story. 'It was a very graceful dance and more importantly, very well placed in the story. When I started shooting for the dance I almost felt as if I belonged to that era,' she sighs.

She says it has taken a long time but Hindi cinema has evolved in recent times. In content and technology, new directors have revolutionized the entertainment business. Writers are relooking at characters and relationships. 'For this, part of the credit ought to go to Ravi Chopra and *Baghbaan*. He had the courage to make a film about an older couple and present them so glamorously. Who would have imagined that Amitabh Bachchan and I would at this stage of our career get to perform so many dance numbers. '*Holi khele Raghuveera Avadh mein* … ', '*Meri makhna* … *meri soniye* … ' besides '*Chali chali* … ' where I made a brief appearance. We even did waltz dancing in a small sequence, which was very enjoyable. There was no awkwardness even though Amitji and I were coming together after almost a decade … ,' she smiles pleasantly.

The success of *Baghbaan* paved the way for Yash Chopra casting them together again in *Veer Zaara,* wherein he made them perform a *lodi* dance with Shah Rukh Khan and Preity Zinta. 'When I arrived on the sets in Punjab and had to start learning the bhangra steps, there was a feeling of déjà vu. It was almost as if time had stood still all these years. I sometimes feel we tend to overemphasize age. Talent has nothing to do with growing old. Cricketers do not forget the game when they retire, nor do boxers forget punching, so why do we assume that artistes will not look attractive on screen just because they have added on years …?'

In *Baabul* Hema has a foot tapping number with Amitabh Bachchan and Salman Khan. In Yash Raj's new film she performs a mujra composed in Kathak choreography. Says Hema, 'After "*Jhhote naina bole* ..." in Lekin this is my first solo dance on screen. It's strange that even now when I get into my costume and take cue for the music, I can feel the adrenaline rushing ...'

Terms of Endearment

Motherhood may be the most exhilarating experience in a woman's life, but in show business, it mars the status of a heroine. Until recently, a heroine was considered fortunate if she succeeded at the box office after matrimony. But post-motherhood, even if she is in the best of shape, she no longer figures in the fantasy of her audience. The very same filmmakers, who stated that mega projects like *Meera* and *Razia Sultan* were inconceivable without Hema Malini, were now apprehensive about casting her after the birth of her first baby.

Call it bad times, but the income tax department slapped a hefty levy, close to Rs 1 crore on the actress. With the passing away of her father, older brother Kannan on a posting in Calcutta, and Jagannath weighed down with his new pharmaceutical business, the actress was facing tough times. Jagan tried his best to be of help but the complications were beyond his knowledge or reach. As months went by the problems multiplied. This is common in show business where the stars are always too busy to inquire about their investments. Hema was no exception. The first thing

Facing Page: *Hema in a still from* Khushboo.

she did was to transfer her files from Madras to Bombay. Her new chartered accountants, P.N. Shah and Sunil Gupta, advised Hema to somehow pay up the penalty and get it out of the way. The only way she could earn that kind of money was by continuing to sign films. The big banners were apparently not interested. The parallel cinema was unsure of approaching her. So she could only choose from what was offered, small budget projects that were completed on time and fetched prompt payments.

Shyam Ralhan's *Ramkali* was the first amongst them. It was Hema's first B-grade movie in box office parlance. For the first time a Hema Malini poster was put up at small-time theatres in distant suburbs. The film starred Hema in a double role as a village belle and a rifle-toting dacoit. Shatrughan Sinha and Suresh Oberoi were her co-stars. Hema had earlier worked with Shatrughan Sinha in *Bhai Ho To Aisa* where he played a villain. The success of *Ramkali* began a new phase of action roles for the star. Hema is the only Hindi film female actor to have done serious sword-fighting and rifle-shooting scenes. She has beaten up Amrish Puri with her ghungroos, Vijayendra Ghatge with a whip, Roopesh Kumar with a tennis racquet and another villain with a table lamp. As recently as in *Baghbaan,* Hema beats up the villain for eveteasing her granddaughter.

The audience enjoyed watching Hema in vendetta sagas and distributors encouraged these projects because of an initial success. After *Seeta Aur Geeta* and *Sholay,* B. Subhash projected her as Fearless Nadia in *Aandhi Toofan.* Later, producer S.K. Kapoor made *Durga,* and soon started a trend for smaller banners to launch dacoit films. Curiously, Hema was the only heroine opposite whom leading heroes like Jeetendra, Shatrughan Sinha and Rajesh Khanna did not mind playing second fiddle. She acknowledged their cooperation but the unprecedented success of these films brought Hema no joy. Once a top-grade actor, she says she felt belittled doing these kind of movies. 'I knew I had compromised with my standards but in the given circumstances, it was the only recourse I could take. I needed the money and I

The Second Coming: Hema in a still from Ramkali.

was reluctant to ask Dharamji for help. My self-respect would not allow it. It was not fair. It was my mess and I had to find a way out of it on my own.'

The nightmare lasted ten years. But after a number of insignificant films and dance performances in India and abroad, Hema gradually managed to clear her debts. 'I learnt the biggest lesson of life ... No matter how busy one gets, no matter how boring the details, professionals must take charge of their own accounts. Never trust money matters to an outsider. One must personally supervise everything that the chartered accountant passes on to you. It is a problem most creative people face, particularly artistes. And by the time we discover the mess, the damage is irreversible,' she advises.

Hema regrets not inquiring after her investments or learning about her finances till it was too late. 'If I was warned at the right time may be I could have prevented the mess. Then, I would not have been as frightened when the calamity struck! Everything has a time and place in life, and one must learn to respect the rhythm of nature.' She regrets rushing through a three-decade career without ever stopping to give enough thought to the innumerable opportunities that presented themselves. 'The biggest banners offered me the choicest roles but there was no one to guide me or help me prepare for a role. Only some filmmakers like Gulzar saab made the effort and the result was evident in my performances,' she reflects.

Perhaps that is the tragedy of stardom. Most of the time, actors go through their long careers without pausing to ponder its impact on their personal lives. The most memorable performance usually is just another day of shooting on another set. Sometimes, actors carry bits of their cherished characters home. But at the end of the year, the memories turn sepia, buried and forgotten under the pressures of new roles and new anxieties. The bottom line is that the show must go on.

Today, when Hema watches some of her old films she feels that she could have played them better, 'In *Sapno Ka Saudagar* particularly, I feel I was too theatrical but I was only doing what my director Mahesh Kaul asked of me. Maybe he wanted that particular image and therefore cast me. In fact what appealed about *Sapno Ka Saudagar* was a young girl getting cheeky with a legendary star. The audience found the relationship refreshing. As artistes, we have to accept what we are told,' she admits.

Of the 100-odd films in which Hema Malini starred, her choices could be divided between the commercial and the creative. Compared to any other heroine of her generation, she enjoyed the maximum number of successes during her time. Beginning with *Johnny Mera Naam, Andaaz, Seeta Aur Geeta, Jugnu, Haath Ki Safai, Prem Nagar, Dharmatma, Sholay* and *Trishul* in the 1970s to *Do Aur Do Paanch, Naseeb, Satte Pe Satta, Rajput, Andha Kanoon* in the 1980s, right up to the latest *Baghbaan* in 2003, her record of hits at the box office is rather enviable.

'Our problem is that we value opportunities only in retrospect,' muses Hema. 'When I was doing these films, it was never with the intention that they could turn out to be milestones someday. At that point I was so caught up with the pressures of day-to-day shooting, putting on wigs and make-up, learning my lines and dance steps. It is only now that I realize how fortunate I was to be essaying so many interesting roles. The current heroines are not as fortunate. Films today have little emphasis on the story. They shoot in exotic locations, wear beautiful costumes, sing sexy songs but their roles are far from memorable,' she opines.

She has warm memories of S. Mukherjee's *Abhinetri* and says that even though her director and hero Shashi Kapoor were her seniors, they treated her like an equal. 'I accepted the film because I liked my role of a dancer and I realized that being a dancer helped me as an actress. *Abhinetri* was my first mature role, as a new bride and being still young I was shy of enacting the honeymoon scenes with my hero. Subodhji and Shashi Kapoor realized my awkwardness and helped me shed my inhibitions. It was a complex character and the film had many layers besides of course some extraordinary music. It is a pity that the film did not fare well at the box office. Over the years, I got used to the idea that films I enjoyed doing need not necessarily fare well commercially. I empathized with the dancer in *Abhinetri* even if I was too young to understand the complexities of marriage. I sympathized with the husband's character as well and admired the courage of the mother-in-law portrayed by Nirupa Roy,' she says.

Hema was fortunate that beginning with *Johnny Mera Naam* (1970), to *Andaaz* (1971), *Seeta Aur Geeta* (1972), *Jugnu* (1973), *Haath Ki Safai* and *Prem Nagar* (1974), *Dharmatma* and *Sholay* (1975), *Mehbooba* (1976), *Azaad* (1977), and to *Trishul* (1978) she was delivering a super hit every year. She was privileged to be offered a variety of roles with directors experimenting with different genres. She was timid and shy in *Jahaan Pyaar Mile*, mischievous in *Waaris*, romantic in *Abhinetri*, running scared in *Aansoo Aur Muskaan* and flamboyant in *Tum Haseen Main Jawan*. Every decade offered her landmark projects escalating her a few rungs higher up the ladder of stardom.

Ramesh Sippy's *Andaaz* generated a lot of interest because Rajesh Khanna, a rage those days was coming together with the

Dream Girl for the first time. Filmmaker Ramesh Sippy had signed Shammi Kapoor as the hero and for the heroine wanted somebody without a definite image. Hema displayed the rare quality to take risks. 'Rameshji was trying to bend rules of mainstream cinema and I wanted to encourage him but frankly what was attractive to me was my flashback in the film featuring Rajesh Khanna. The entire sequence was so energetic and fabulously shot, particularly the accident scene. The audience was unprepared for the turning point. That Rajesh Khanna was the superstar at that time, added to the magic,' she asserts.

It is said that when filmmaker F.C. Mehra was casting his costume drama *Lal Pathar* his original choice for the 'other' woman was Vyjayanthimala. The hero Raaj Kumar, however, was very keen that it should be Hema Malini. F.C. Mehra was unsure if Hema, still a newcomer then, would be able to portray such a complex role. But Raaj Kumar was persistent. When finally Mehra approached Hema, those close to her tried to poison her against the role. They said it would be a mistake to accept a negative character pitched opposite Raakhee, who had been signed to play the role of the protagonist's wife.

Raaj Kumar suspected that Hema would be misled and personally visited her to persuade her to do the role. Recalls Hema, 'He was a major star at that time, while I was just a newcomer. But he made the effort to come and explain the merit of the role. He advised that I must watch the original Bangla film, *Lal Pathor,* starring Uttam Kumar and Supriya Devi before taking any decision. I did just that and needed no more convincing. I had made up my mind.'

When they began shooting for the film, Raaj Kumar guided the young actress at every stage. 'He was all the time watching over me and telling me when I was going wrong. I was very grateful for all his suggestions,' says Hema gratefully. As the shooting progressed, director Sushil Majumdar was convinced that Hema was the right choice for the role. He wanted the character to portray all the *navrasas* and Hema being a dancer, the

Lal Pathar: *A complex role portrayed so beautifully and convincingly.*

role was easy for her. 'My favourite scene in the film is where I stand beside the tiger consumed with rage and envy. For this film I received maximum appreciation from my colleagues. Many of my co-stars wrote me congratulatory notes about my performance, which made me feel very special. How strange that in all the films I did thereafter I never played someone as complex or passionate,' she wonders.

Released in 1971, *Naya Zamana* was an inspiring film where for the first time three veteran writers: Promod Chakraborty, Sachin Bhowmick and Gulshan Nanda jointly worked on the screenplay. The story of a young man's vision of a utopian world, it dealt with the theme of fading idealism. The climax portrayed villain Pran publishing Dharmendra's novel in his name. The idea was similar to Rehman publishing Guru Dutt's poetry as his own in the 1950s classic *Pyaasa*.

In *Paraya Dhan* Hema plays a foster daughter, in *Tere Mere Sapne* a film star, in *Raja Jaani* a street dancer. The same Shridhar, who had thrown out Hema from his Tamil film before she got her break in Hindi films, offered her *Gehri Chaal*. After her stardom Shridhar had no qualms about approaching her for his film and

Hema consented gracefully. Though launched much earlier, the film was released after *Seeta Aur Geeta*. There is a story that the exhibitors refused to buy the film unless the filmmaker included some action shots of Hema. The director had no choice but to change the script halfway through the film and shoot the climax with his heroine bashing up the villain instead of heroes Jeetendra and Amitabh Bachchan. Hema was as convincing as a village belle (*Patthar Aur Payal*) as a city pickpocket (*Amir Garib*).

Hema in a still from Palkon Ki Chaon Mein.

About Nagi Reddy's *Prem Nagar* she says, 'I played Rajesh Khanna's secretary, Lata. I could identify with the character because she is proud and restrained.' Hema says she looked forward to outdoor shootings in Madras for that was the only way she could get time to spend in her newly built bungalow. 'Otherwise with my hectic schedule I would seldom find opportunities to enjoy my new home. So every time I was offered interesting South projects, I accepted them immediately. The family looked forward to my shootings in Madras because we could all be together and spend quality time.'

Dulhan was a typical family drama where Hema transforms from a radiant bride to a reluctant widow. In the film, Hema's performance had to come full circle. 'It was a good story and the director did a competent job of it. I particularly like the way the title song "*Mein dulhan teri tu dulha piya ...*" is picturized and it was highly appreciated.'

Hema says everything about Gulzar's *Khushboo* was just perfect. The characterization, the timing of the film, the casting and most important the costumes. This was the first time Hema was draped in cotton-crumpled saris with unmatched blouses, her hair tied in a simple braid and her face devoid of any make-up. Based on Sarat Chandra's story *Pandit Moshai*, the film proved a milestone in Hema's career. She says, 'Only Gulzar saab can be so simple and yet effective. All the characters were so beautifully etched out. I could very easily identify with my character Kusum. Her quest for self-respect at the cost of self-denial is almost tragic. I feel sad every time I watch this film,' she reminisces with a sigh.

Feroze Khan was obsessed with the subject of *Dharmatma*. Hema recalls that his intensity was infectious on the sets. 'While shooting in Afghanistan he was like a man possessed and this reflects in his magnificent canvas. *Dharmatma* was a very glamorous film, very well mounted and I was presented with a lot of panache. Undoubtedly it is my most flamboyant character in films. There is a bounce to her, a raw energy that is missed when she dies in the second half. Feroze Khan was so smitten with the character that throughout the shooting he would address me as "Reshma" to an extent that at one stage I began to believe I was an Afghan girl living in those hills. Parmeshwar Godrej designed the costumes of the film. I think this is the only time she has designed for a film and only because the director was a personal friend.'

When Ramesh Sippy narrated the role of Basanti in *Sholay*, Hema was not at all impressed. She could not fathom why the director wanted to cast her as a *tangewali*. But after two successes (*Andaaz* and *Seeta Aur Geeta*) it was difficult for her to refuse him. 'I agreed half-heartedly and would have never forgiven myself had I turned down the role. After the release of *Sholay* wherever I went I was identified as Basanti … People wanted to know how I rattled those dialogues … Learning the long lines and delivering them in one "take" was a nightmare, but Rameshji helped me … Also the fact that I have a good memory,' she adds smiling brightly.

Sanyasi is rated as Hema's ultimate glamorization on screen. With Hema playing the seductress who had to seduce the ascetic, dress designer Bhanu Athaiya was instructed to spend lavishly on her costumes. Hema says she thoroughly enjoyed dressing up in those elaborate costumes and jewellery, and cameraman Radhu Karmakar as always did full justice to her beauty. 'It's very important for an actor to relate to his/her cameraman and the other way round. Though actors communicate very little with the technicians as compared to the directors, their contribution cannot be undermined.'

Hema was at an interesting phase of her career. If she was playing the ambitious career woman in the southern remake *Sunehra Sansar* on one hand, on the other she was a princess in *Mehbooba*. She was an airhostess in *Aap Beeti* and a dancer in *Kinara*. Understandably the ratio of successes over the years was decreasing. *Do Thug, Dhoop Chaon, Palkon Ki Chaon Mein, Dillagi* to name a few were mere averages.

In Yash Chopra's *Trishul*, Hema was cast as an entrepreneur. In the film, hero Shashi Kapoor who plays a young tycoon has to attend an official meeting and is pleasantly surprised that his associate is a woman. For this film, costume designer Bhanu Athaiya dressed Hema in short hair and chiffon saris worn with a sleeveless blouse. It was a small but a delicious role and the character was eminently likeable. 'In her dressing and her behaviour she was a contrast to the conventional heroine I had portrayed so far,' analyses Hema.

Many years ago, B.R. Films had signed Hema for a period film *Chanakya Chandragupt* that never got made. Hema regretted missing the opportunity of working with Dilip Kumar. So when Manoj Kumar approached her for *Kranti*, she agreed instantly. 'Dilip saab and I had some important scenes together and it was an enchanting experience watching the thespian at work. I felt great regard for my character Princess Meenakshi in the film. It calls for courage to give up your throne and entrust your heart to your enemy. She did and that made the character very special.' Hema says that Manoj Kumar had a unique style in his placement of camera. 'As a director he had the ability of shooting very lengthy scenes and songs in just one shot. This was taxing for the actors while shooting but the advantage was that the shot got over in one take and that saved a lot of time on the sets.'

For years Hema remained the first choice of all the big banners. B.R. Chopra's *The Burning Train*, F.C. Mehra's *Ali Baba Aur 40 Chor*, Manmohan Desai's *Naseeb*, Ramanand Sagar's *Bagawat* and Ramesh Sippy's *Satte Pe Satta*. She was the first choice of all the independent directors as well. Rakesh Kumar's *Do Aur Do Paanch*, Subhash Ghai's *Krodhi*, Chetan Anand's *Kudrat* to name a few. It is to her credit that she juggled the more artistic *Ratnadeep*, *Jyoti* and *Dard* with mainstream movies like *Bandish, Aas Paas* and *Samrat* with equal ease and elan.

In 1977 Jaya Chakravarti produced *Swami* directed by Basu Chatterjee. The original casting of the film was to be Hema Malini and Manoj Kumar, but since Hema had no spare dates Jaya thought it would be safer to make a smaller budget film with an affordable star cast. And signed Shabana Azmi and Girish Karnad instead. Hema and Dharmendra did an item number in the film. She had loved the story and the presentation and promised Basu Chatterjee that some day, when she had free dates, they would do a similar project together.

Dard was inspired by the Ashok Kumar-Suchitra Sen famous bilingual starrer, *Mamta*. A striking tale of love and sacrifice, Hema played Ashok Kumar's role while Rajesh Khanna did Suchitra Sen's double role. She has no specific memories related to the film but remembers the scene when the hero suggests that she deliberately lose the case so that his son, a rising lawyer, may win. 'It was a very well-written and emotionally charged scene,' she says.

Looking back now, Hema says some films did not impress during narration but surprised her in the final outcome. *Jyoti* was a remake of *Bahurani,* starring Guru Dutt and Mala Sinha in the original. 'For the first time I was playing a fiery housewife and I enjoyed beating up the villain with a whip. So did the audience. After all, why must it always be the men who do all the bashing up on the screen?' she asks prettily. Inspired from the celebrated Bangla novel *Swayam Sidha*, the subject was very close to director Promod Chakraborty's heart. 'He wanted to make this film for a long time and whenever Chakida spoke about it, he would become very emotional. It has been my observation that if the director is emotionally attached to his subject, the film holds a special magic. My character Gauri is married off to a retarded man who she gradually nurses to normalcy. There was a powerful message in the film that if you dare, you can. Gauri dared and was able to change her destiny,' she says expansively.

Hema states that after a certain age, stars should be careful about the projects they accept because Hindi cinema has a way of stereotyping actors. *Meri Aawaz Suno* and *Ek Naya Itihaas* were interesting subjects and released around the same time but failed

Dard: *A striking tale of love and sacrifice. (Hema seen here with Rajesh Khanna).*

to make an impact on the audience. *Justice Choudhary,* she feels was a learning experience. In the film her hero Jeetendra starred in a double role as the husband and later as Hema's son, while she was depicted growing old. 'I did not enjoy wearing the white wigs and the wrinkles on my face. After that, I made sure not to accept similar roles again,' she grimaces.

Andhaa Kanoon, produced by A. Purnachandra Rao and directed by T. Rama Rao, was a super hit all over India. This was the first time Hema appeared as a police inspector and played sister to South superstar Rajnikanth playing a criminal. Earlier she had also played sister to Amitabh Bachchan in *Gehri Chaal.* In Hindi films it is usually believed that if the lead pair is cast as brother-sister they will not be later accepted as a romantic pair. 'Amitabh and I started with a brother-sister casting and went on to do several romantic films later on in our career,' says Hema.

Spreading Her Wings

Hema thought of her debut film production when she was reading Irwing Wallace's *The Second Lady*. 'The scenes played before my eyes and I could not put the book down. That is the time I told Dharamji that I would launch my own banner very soon,' she reveals. *Sharara* produced by her brother Jagannath under the banner of Angel Films was released in 1984 and starred Hema, Raaj Kumar, Shatrughan Sinha and Mithun Chakraborty. The film did not fare well at the box office but was appreciated for its production standards and the gripping plot.

Thus encouraged, Hema was inspired to launch her first teleserial *Noopur* produced by HM Video Creations in 1990. It was about a classical dancer who is cheated by her travel agent and aided by a stranger, played by Kabir Bedi, presents her debut show against all odds. Her performance, however, does not live up to the expectations of her critics. To improve on her art she travels to the dance city Tanjore in search of a guru. After months of rigorous training she returns to retrieve her lost glory and fans.

The story was Hema's concept and scripted by Gulzar. Since this was the first time Gulzar was writing about the life of a

Facing Page: *Creatively inclined, Hema was always open to new ideas and challenges. In a still from TV serial* Kamini-Damini

Television is addictive: A scene from Doordarshan's teleserial Noopur. *Based on the life of a dancer this serial became a big hit with the masses.*

dancer, he wanted to make sure that he got all the references right. He asked Hema to send him relevant books on this art form. His familiarity with Hema's family background and lifestyle helped him to compose a sensitive screenplay with realistic characters that made it easy for Hema to identify with her role.

Vikas Desai was Hema's first choice for director. She had earlier done *Terah Panne* with him, but somehow things didn't work out. Later, she approached several directors but could not decide who to choose. Says Hema, 'I was very clear that it had to be someone who understood classical dance because we had planned to introduce different classical dance forms in every episode. We talked to many people and waited for months but failed to find the right person. Finally, Gulzar saab suggested that I direct the serial myself. It was his idea that out of the 22-minute-episode we reserve six minutes for dance. I was not sure how the audience would accept that but Gulzar saab insisted that if the serial was about dance we should not be apologetic about it. We went along with his conviction and he was proved right. To confirm that we were on the right track, for one particular episode we deliberately excluded dance and we discovered that the viewers were disappointed. Interestingly, after all these years, wherever I go people always compliment me for *Noopur*. Even those who have no connection with classical dance like a sardarji I met abroad, asked me why I could not make a sequel to *Noopur* … Shooting the serial was not easy for me. This was the first time I was acting, dancing, directing and also producing. Handling so many departments was a draining exercise. When the serial ended, I took off on a long holiday to London. I thought I would never do another serial again but television is addictive. Once you have been into it, you want to do it over and over again,' she laughs.

Alongside her experiments with the small screen Hema's tryst with the big screen continued even though her later releases lacked the zing of her earlier films. She was fortunate that her recent films did not dull her image in the minds of her devoted fans. 'There is a silver lining to the darkest cloud … ' says Hema philosophically. 'The good thing about my bad phase was that I was suddenly accessible to parallel filmmakers. I now had the opportunity of working with new directors like Sukhwant Dhadda in *Ek Chadar Maili Si* and Aruna Raje in *Rihaee*. Those were liberating experiences, both as an actress and as a woman,' discloses Hema. Initially Hema was reluctant to accept *Ek Chadar Maili Si* because Dharmendra had unpleasant memories associated with the subject. Many years ago veteran actress Geeta Bali had died of smallpox while shooting the film by the same title and Dharmendra cast as Geeta Bali's brother-in-law was a witness to the tragedy. He felt superstitious about Hema doing a movie on the same subject, and that was also the reason why no producer over the years had attempted to make a film on the subject again. Sukhwant Dhadda did and Hema cast as protagonist broke the jinx.

She knew she was going to do *Rihaee* when Aruna Raje narrated the story to her. 'All round the world, it is always women who cope with domestic and social crises and yet they are considered the weaker sex. This was the first film where I played an adulteress, who protests when the husband forces her to abort her lover's baby. It was breaking away from the traditional image I had so far,' she explains. The unit of *Rihaee* has amusing anecdotes about truckloads of villagers arriving at their shooting only to have a look at the glorious diva Hema Malini. She was the only star in the unit and the rest of the cast comprised television and theatre artistes.

Critics acknowledged her choices as an actor. It coincided with her return to some of the big camps. Hema signed Yash Chopra's *Vijay* and Ramoji Rao's *Jamaai Raja.* 'I accepted the role of the mother-in-law because I found her interesting. I thought it would be different to project someone supremely stupid like her. But the trade automatically assumed that I was transitioning to mother roles and put me in a senior bracket, which was very annoying. Why do we assume that a heroine past her prime can only play mother characters? Do not older women have a life and a story? It is indeed sad that we are so restricted by our vision,' she sighs.

Having experienced the other cinema, Hema was no longer willing to play second fiddle only to be a part of the mainstream. 'I preferred featuring in smaller, meaningful roles that were more challenging. I loved my role in *Lekin* where I turn old, waiting for my younger sister's spirit. It was a haunting role and appeared in flashbacks and flash-forwards. Hridayanath Mangeshkar's music in the film was simply mesmerizing,' she relates.

After much deliberation Hema took the plunge and launched herself as a feature film director. The pre-production to the shooting handled by cousin Mohan was almost complete. The film was ready to go on the floor but Hema had still not found her hero. She was visiting Hyderabad for her show and like always telephoned Ma Indiraji to seek her blessings before her

Hema portrayed a meaningful and satisfying role in Ek Chadar Maili Si.

performance. Ma casually inquired on the progress of her film and Hema bemoaned that she had yet to find a hero. 'Don't worry, you will find him soon and he will be the biggest star,' Ma said in her characteristic cheerful tone.

Hema wasn't convinced but as destined, on her return to Mumbai, she was surfing television channels when she spotted Shah Rukh Khan in *Fauji*. He looked refreshing and seemed to have the potential to become a film hero. Hema asked her office to make inquiries and discovered that he lived in Delhi. Her cousin Prabha contacted him but he refused to believe that Hema Malini would phone him. He insisted that somebody was playing a prank on him. An exasperated Prabha left her number with him, asking him to call back. He did and spoke directly with Hema.

Two days later Shah Rukh Khan arrived at Hema's home in Mumbai for an audition. Hema was already familiar with his acting and after meeting him approved of his appearance. There was only one problem – his mop of hair covered his entire face. A bit shyly, Hema asked him if he could do something about his hair. Shah Rukh ran his fingers quickly through his hair. He looked better than before but still not satisfactory. Hema called her make-up man to push Shah Rukh's hair back with gel. The transformation was amazing. While all this was happening, Dharmendra walked in. Hema introduced him to her discovery, and said she was considering taking him as the hero. He endorsed her choice and Shah Rukh Khan was confirmed for the role.

'Nobody knew at that time that Shah Rukh was going to become such a big star, but Ma had foreseen it,' says Hema with a broad smile. 'That is the power of great souls. They view things from a higher perspective, forewarn us about the happenings and then detach themselves.'

A grand mahurat was held at a suburban hotel where Hema announced the film. The title *Dil Aashna Hai* was suggested by Ma Indiraji, also a very competent writer in Urdu and English who has to her credit several books. It was out of choice that this poetess had decided to live a life of a saint. Adapted from Shirley Conran's popular novel *Lace,* the subject revolved around female bonding. It was an enjoyable experience for Hema to spend time with her four heroines, Dimple Kapadia, Amrita Singh, Sonu Walia and Divya Bharati. 'It was a different mood when the heroes came on the sets but I must say that all of them were extremely supportive. As an actress it was interesting for me to watch emotions from behind the camera rather than be in front of it,' she narrates.

During the making of *Dil Aashna Hai* Hema discovered that direction was a demanding job. 'I was confident of extracting good performances from my artistes and always arrived on the sets well prepared. Often when I would be sitting by myself, reflecting on my next shot, my spot boy would suggest that I go and rest in my van. Though I had graduated to being a director he treated me like an actor, but how could I isolate myself when my head was buzzing with ideas? I guess that is the difference between an actor and a director. For an actor, the involvement ends with his scene. For a filmmaker, on the other hand, every shot is his life, his own canvas,' she elaborates.

'It was the first time I understood the virtue of patience. So far I had taken all my directors for granted but after *Dil Aashna Hai* I looked at them with a new respect,' she adds.

The film was released in 1991 and would have fared well at the box office had the communal riots not broken out in the city. Hema remembers that she was performing her new ballet *Durga* at Rang Sharda Theatre in Bandra where Bal Thackerey was the chief guest. After the show, Thackerey advised her to leave immediately and even provided security to escort her home. The next day, the city was up in flames. Distributors advised Hema to retract the delivery from the exhibitors and postpone the release until the riots had subsided. But it was too late to withdraw. The following week *Dil Aashna Hai* was released to a weak opening in theatres all over. Hema learnt her first big lesson as a filmmaker. 'It's not sufficient to make a good film. Equally important is to have the release at the right time,' she says sagaciously.

Her debut as a director was yet another turning point in Hema's career. Now producers approached her with directorial assignments. But Hema was in no hurry to make any commitments. She bided her time for her next move. From a distance, she watched her discoveries Shah Rukh Khan and Divya Bharati scale greater heights. She revelled in the compliments that came her way. A year passed by and Hema had made up her mind.

The year was 1994 and she announced her first telefilm *Mohini* for Zee TV. Inspired from Malayatoor Ramakrishnan's Malayalam novel *Yaksh*, the film revolved around a professor who suspects that his wife is a witch. 'It was a tempestuous love story of a married couple,' recalls Hema. Around this time director Kawal Sharma signed up Hema for a mega television project on Rani Laxmibai, titled *Jhansi Ki Rani*, that was launched amidst much fanfare but shelved later.

The same year, she signed a freedom saga *Yug*, to be directed by Sunil Agnihotri. The original contract was for 113 episodes but Hema became restless and discontinued soon after. 'It was the phase when television was becoming very important but as a performer I was uncomfortable with the medium.' Hema used her spare dates to launch another serial titled *Women of India* that featured both historical and contemporary women characters. Devoting eight episodes to each character, Hema starred in the premier episode *Amrapali* because this character of the Magadh court dancer had always fascinated her. 'I had seen Vyjayanthimala's film on the subject released in the 1960s and loved it immensely. It was my dream to play the character, and since I could not play the character on the big screen I played her in a teleserial.'

Women of India was produced and directed by Hema. *Urvashi* was one of the other episodes of the serial and starred her cousin Prabha. There were demands for more episodes by the channel but Hema got fed up of the endless shootings and the round-the-clock editing schedules. Her daughters were growing up and she needed to spend more time with them. To compartmentalize her life, Hema decided to hire a full-time director. She continued as a producer though. Ravi Chopra took over the directorial reins with *Jhansi Ki Rani* and continued till the end of 56 episodes. Hema relished the creative break while her cousin Mohan Raghavan expertly shouldered all production responsibilities.

By now a veteran on the small screen, Hema launched a women's helpline, *Aap Ki Saheli,* on Doordarshan. The programme though completely different in content was in a way inspired by the highly successful Hindi magazine *Meri Saheli* – *New Woman* in English, published by Pioneer Publications, that she edited. Hema cherishes her experience with the print media. She says her frequent interaction with the editorial team sensitized her to women issues, both in rural and urban India. She particularly reveres her association with the magazine owners Rajiv and Pinky Pahwa. 'It was because of their trust in me that I was able to shoulder the responsibility.' *Aap Ki Saheli* ran for 150 episodes in the form of a daily programme. What lured the channels to Hema Malini was that her sheer presence guaranteed high TRPs for the serial. Doordarshan's most popular programme

Rangoli recorded its highest TRP ratings during the 162 weeks when Hema hosted the show.

Filmmaker Ramanand Sagar, well known for his popular serial *Ramayan,* signed Hema for his next mythological serial *Jai Durga* because he felt she had the personality to project the powerful goddess. She agreed, because she is fascinated with the mother goddess. But she backed out when she realized that her producer had too many pre-conditions. Hema felt uncomfortable signing a contract with so many restrictions. But she was destined to play the goddess because weeks after her fallout with the Sagars, actor Puneet Issar, making his directorial debut, offered her Cinevista's *Jai Mata ki.* The role called for her to don the various incarnations of goddess Amba. 'I loved the idea of playing Lakshmi, Durga and Saraswati because I knew everyone would identify with the characters. That the producer gave me complete freedom was a further incentive. I cannot work under pressure. It's only when I'm at ease that I'm able to perform my best,' she states.

It is to her credit that despite her innumerable acting assignments and dance shows, her home banner continued to produce teleserials looked after by cousin Mohan. She is probably Hindi cinema's only actress to produce two Marathi serials, *Songti,* about the experiences of three friends, a police officer, a politician and a journalist; and *Umbartha,* about a widow's attempt to find a place in society.

Hema was comfortably settled in the television world when southern superstar Kamal Haasan offered her a role in his home production *Hey! Ram.* Kamal originally wanted to cast Hema and Esha as mother-daughter, but finding Hema not eager to launch Esha as yet he cast only Hema as Vasundhara Das's mother. After their romantic lead in *Ek Nayi Paheli* (1984) the two were coming together after more than a decade. This time as mother and son-in-law. Hema says she accepted the film because it marked Kamal Haasan's debut as a director. 'I have no false notions about my age. I'm a mother in real life and have no hang-ups about playing mother on screen provided I'm portrayed realistically.' In the same year her co-star Vinod Khanna asked her to do his home production *Himalayputra* launching his son Akshaye Khanna. In a way, the two films marked her second innings.

'That was a time when I was flooded with offers to do mother roles and I steadfastly refused all offers. It was because I was so firm in my decision and able to resist their pressures that I was considered worthy to be offered *Baghbaan*,' points out Hema triumphantly. When Ravi Chopra visited Hema's home to narrate the story of *Baghbaan*, Jaya Chakravarti though unwell, sat up for the entire story session. When Ravi Chopra left, Jaya asked her daughter if she intended doing the film. Not sure what exactly was on her mother's mind, Hema said that she was happy spending time at home and not seriously inclined. 'I said so because I felt that Amma was feeling insecure about having me out of her sight. She took a long pause, and then said that declining this offer would be a mistake. "You just cannot pass by such an offer. A role like this opposite Amitabh Bachchan should not be lost," she surmised wisely.'

Hema had no doubts that she would do the film considering her long association with the B.R. banner and with Ravi Chopra as a director. That her mother approved of this role was doubly reassuring. And that the film starred her old hero Amitabh Bachchan was an added bonus. The most important reason, however, was that it was a role of a lifetime. It was a dream role about a dream couple. 'On the first day of shooting at Film City, I was a trifle nervous but it was almost as if Amitji and I had never stopped working together. We had last starred in *Satte Pe Satta* in 1981. Roles like *Baghbaan* don't come everyday. The film is a collage of beautiful moments in the life of an ageing couple,' she concludes.

Riding on the success of *Baghbaan*, the pair did a cameo in Yash Chopra's *Veer Zaara*. 'It was a small role but it was enjoyable because of the star cast. Amitabh and I play a Punjabi couple. Yash Chopra came to me carrying a DVD of *Ek Chadar Maili Si* and said that he wanted the same rustic look for his film.' *Veer Zaara* was shot in Chandigarh and mid-way through the shooting Yashji felt that adding some dialogues in Punjabi would lend flavour to the scenes and therefore Chopra cleverly changed Hema's character to a South Indian married to a Punjabi.

Acting will always remain Hema's passion, but simultaneously she finds herself drawn to other mediums related to acting. She was the first big star to experiment with television. Starting with *Terah Panne* in 1982 where she played prominent characters from history, she continued right up to *Kamini Damini* in 2002. Besides production, direction and dance, Hema is also drawn to sketching and writing. 'I have so many stories brimming in my head. How I wish I had the discipline to script my thoughts or at least can find someone who can write these stories for me. It's my dream to work in a memorable role with Esha and in case no director casts us together I hope I'm able to direct her myself some day ...,' she muses.

Life is coming full circle for Hema Malini. In her matriarchal home where until recently three generations lived together, she was the balancing factor. Providing reassurance to her children she sought the same from her mother. Right until the time she became bedridden, Jaya Chakravarti was always in the auditorium when Hema performed her dance shows. Despite being in frail health and needing assistance, Jaya was always enthusiastic and wanting to participate in her daughter's achievements. Says Hema, 'I'm sure I'll do the same for my daughters ... The reason I emphasize so much on dance is because cinema can never match the satisfaction of a stage performance. In films one works in fragmented phases but on stage you evolve as the character. That is why my father always wanted me to portray heroic women. That is also the reason why the *natyashastra* tradition disciplines dancers to turn vegetarian. If you have noticed, most dancers are extremely religious. I began fasting on Fridays after I started performing *Durga*. Fasting is not about abstinence, it is about willpower ... Just as dance is as much about devotion and spirituality as about art and grace ... '

Dance Like a God

Hema Malini is consistently spell-binding on any public platform because she has been accustomed to show business from a very young age. Performing on stage since the age of six, she has over the years been exposed to various auditoria and audiences in various cities and countries. From the time she can remember, she has been familiar with the microphone and the music. She has grown up surrounded by the sound of applause and the spotlight, the beat of *tatu kazhi* and the tinkling of her anklets, the fragrance of fresh flowers and the alluring costumes. She is well acquainted with the sparkle of her jewellery, the grandeur of her accessories and the splendour of her red-painted hands and feet. She remembers that sinking feeling just before the curtain rises and as a little girl hearing her father's booming voice announcing her name and dance item filling the auditorium. After every show, there was as much talk about Chakravarti's style of compering as of Hema's talent. 'Appa had the gift of the gab, a way with words that could not be matched by anyone until many years later, his own son,' says the proud daughter.

Facing Page: *Dance for Hema is not just a creative expression, it is bhakti. Hema in her ballet* Radha Krishna.

Young as she was, Hema could intuitively decipher a genuine admirer of her dance from a fake fan. As she got older and performed at bigger shows, she became more astute in her judgement of her audience. Her parents and she deliberately opted for smaller, more aware shows sponsored by South Indian organizations than big concerts promoted by unknown people. The Chakravartis prefered modest auditoria to swanky halls packed with star-struck fans. Sometimes though, careful as they were, there were errors of judgement. In the 1970s particularly when Hema was at the zenith of her career there were several instances when show organizers exploited her stardom.

One specific episode that turned memorably unpleasant was when the organizer, to lure bigger audiences, publicized her Bharatanatyam performance as 'Hema Malini Nite'. The publicity gave wrong signals to the audience who expected Hema to perform film dances at the concert. When she continued to perform her classical numbers, some of them turned rowdy and disrupted the show with loud protests for film songs. Though offended, Hema was gracious enough to appear on stage and clarify the misunderstanding. After that, the show went on uninterrupted. 'The incident was a learning experience for me. In all my future shows I was overcautious about how they advertised the concert. It took me some time but gradually I was able to cultivate a more informed audience,' she sums up resolutely.

Interestingly, Hema Malini is the only actress so far who has continued with her dance shows along with her film career. What is even more remarkable is that there was no break in her dance shows post marriage, during pregnancy or even after the birth of children. 'My dance costumes over the years altered from large to moderate, depending on the phase of my life. So have the designs from traditional to haute couture, but the passion remains undiminished. I did not stop dancing even during my pregnancy. In fact nobody ever realized when I was pregnant with Esha because of my cleverly disguised costume. Naturally I was careful not to include very vigorous movements.' The practice was continued even as she carried Ahana. 'Once they grew up, I shed my weight and got back to my old regimen. I continued performing solo Bharatanatyam but deep inside me the artiste was restless and hankered for more,' she elaborates.

The year was 1987, Hema made the customary call to her guruma to seek her blessings. Ma suggested that it was time Hema thought of evolving her dance form. 'Have you thought of performing ballets?' Ma asked Hema. 'May be you should, this is the right time,' she suggested. The words stayed with Hema even though the message seemed like a distant dream. Until one lazy Sunday morning, Hema was in her bedroom, watching Doordarshan, the sole television channel at that time. A dance ballet being performed by the Bharatiya Kala Kendra of Delhi caught her attention. The role of Ram portrayed by a twenty-year-old dancer was particularly impressive. Here was a talented artiste worth meeting, thought Hema. She mentioned this to her chartered accountant, Guptaji.

By sheer coincidence, Guptaji happened to visit the sets of another client, Ramanand Sagar, a few days later, during the shooting of Sagar's popular serial *Ramayan.* Sagar introduced him to a young dancer, Bhushan Lakhandri, who was playing the role of Vishnu. Talking to him, Guptaji discovered that he was the 'Ram' whom Hema had seen and admired on Doordarshan and Guptaji introduced Bhushan to Hema at her Juhu bungalow. It was a meeting that changed two destinies.

Bhushan says he can never forget that meeting. 'We were seated in the living room, waiting for her. I was nervous since this was the first time I was visiting a film star's residence. Then, Hemaji strolled in. She was wearing a green sari and looked gorgeous. Her first sentence to me was, "Aaj hamare ghar bahut bade kalakar aaye hain ... " She said it so spontaneously that it immediately put me at ease. A while later Esha walked into the room and exclaimed, "Ram has come to our home." I was amused. This was a special day in my life,' smiles Lakhandri.

Hema informed Lakhandri that she was keen on performing ballets on stage and wondered if he could create a concept for her. Bhushan asked for three days' time. On the fourth day, he was ready with the script of *Nritya Mallika,* comprising assorted dance items involving a number of artistes. Hema approved of the idea instantly. The duo contacted music director Shaili Dutta in Delhi and music recordings started soon after.

Meera: *'Meera is an extension of my love for my guruma.'*

It was only when she started her rehearsals that Hema realized that this would be the first time she would be performing with other artistes on stage. The thought terrified her. All these years, since the age of six, Hema was used to performing only solo dances. In films she danced with group dancers but it was a different medium. 'The stage is a more intimate territory and I was unaccustomed to invasion in my private space. The ballet called for new adjustments. I had to learn to synchronize with twenty-two other artistes. It was very difficult but Bhushan's expert choreography ensured that our movements were not clumsy …

'The second inhibition was to adjust to the idea of performing to pre-recorded music. So far I was used to dancing to live music – my guru's *nattuvangam.* For years I had taken entry from the right of the stage, walked to the left where my teacher was seated, touched his feet and took centre stage. Throughout the performance, there was an eye contact, a connection with the guru that instilled confidence in me. Now for the first time in so many years, I was learning to perform on recorded music, something we only did in films. It was a big challenge. Bhushan's novel choreography was an inspiration. My first dance item with him was *Ardhanareshwar.* Our combination worked marvellously. Bhushan is a master of Manipuri, Kathak and Odissi while, I'm familiar with Bharatanatyam, Mohini Attam and Kuchipudi. One of the items from *Nritya Mallika* is *Triveni* wherein we combine three different dance forms (Bharatanatyam, Odissi and Kathak) to interpret the three famous rivers of India – Ganga, Jamuna and Saraswati. Whenever we perform this number the response is overwhelming and we are drowned with "encores".'

Their debut ballet *Beggar Princess* written by Sri Dilip Kumar Roy, Ma Indiraji's guru, was the first of its kind in India. 'Classical dance does not appeal to a universal audience, but ballets do, particularly to the rural audience. It's because ballets involve three art forms: dance, drama and music. When these three forms are well synchronized the presentation is successful. When the combination is out of sync, the audience gets restless. Performing artistes need to understand this. Only then can we fight for a rightful place for ballets in entertainment,' analyses Hema.

Hema chose *Meera* because she liked the story of her total surrender to God in the face of adversities. 'The legend describes the circumstances that lead Meera's husband to force her to consume a cup of poison and how she survives this injustice. My love for Meera is an extension of my love for my guruma. She always emphasized on the virtue of surrender. Meera belonged to the sixteenth century but lived life on her terms. Her love for the Lord was selfless and flawless. When I perform this ballet I totally surrender to Meera. I firmly believe that once on stage, she takes over from me and my anguish and my craving for the Lord after that is not mine but Meera's own emotions.'

Hema has an almost profound experience to relate during the music recording of the ballet at Sunny Sound Studio in Juhu. 'All of us were engrossed in the music when suddenly I was permeated with chandan fragrance. The aroma was mysterious because recording rooms don't allow visitors, and my mother and the music director too confirmed my doubts. We tried to rationalize that someone must have lit sandalwood incense sticks in the adjoining room, but nothing of that sort had happened. There is a deeper meaning to the episode. It sounds surrealistic but I strongly believe there was a supreme presence amidst us in the room that day.'

Hema's quest for perfection continued. Interestingly, *Meera* is Natyavihar Kala Kendra's only ballet to be choreographed in Kathak because Bharatanatyam, Hema opines, would have been an inappropriate dance form to represent Meera who hails from Northern India. Similarly when she thought of staging *Ramayan*, she contacted film music director Ravindra Jain because she felt his vast knowledge in mythology and soulful music would contribute to the ballet. Since then Jain has become an integral part of Natyavihar Kala Kendra. Hema elaborates that the *Ramayan* is very vast and there are many versions. 'Our ballet is

Ramayan: *'We focus on the love and romance of Ram and Sita ... (a) relationship of perfect love and compatibility.'*

inspired from *Ramcharitmanas*. There is much more to the Ram-Sita relationship than just Ram's betrayal and Sita's trial by fire. Our ballet begins with Ram's childhood, then his romance in the Pushpvatika followed by the Sita *Swayamwar*, right up to their exile. We focus on their romance rather than their travesties. Ram and Sita are the ideal couple. Their relationship is made up of perfect love and compatibility,' she elucidates.

The epic is an integral part of Indian heritage. Written by Tulsidas, *Ramayan* is the story of a man so virtuous that he came to be revered as God. 'The epic dictates a code of moral and social conduct for the humanity. I personally believe that it is very important that all dancers participating in my ballet understand the essence of the epic. I make sure that before we begin rehearsals all of them relate to the subject and the implication of their roles. Very often we have young actors from different religions who don't have sufficient knowledge and understanding of their characters. We had a young actor, Anthony, chosen to play

Hanuman because of his physique. He was a restless boy, all the time jumping from one corner to another. So I sat him down and explained the power of Lord Hanuman to him. On his first show I personally supervised his dressing and tied the anklet on his foot. The exercise is important because the actor needs to connect with the philosophy of the ballet.'

To her surprise Hema discovered that the actors became emotionally attached to the ballet and possessive about their roles. 'We have artistes who started young with us, got engaged, married, had babies but still continue with the shows. Their involvement is touching. The Sita *bidai* scene for some mysterious reason remains the eternal tearjerker. Irrespective of who plays the part of Sita's father Janak, the actor always breaks into tears in the scene. The first time it happened I thought the actor was going

Durga: '*When I perform the Kali rampage I'm startled by my own energy ...*'

through some personal problem. But since then it has occured so many times that we have all got used to the emotional breakdown.'

Ramayan was Hema's first ballet when the Natyavihar Kala Kendra was invited to stage shows all over America. Hema has an interesting anecdote related to the ballet and her guruma. Before leaving for her long journey she spoke to her guruma to seek her blessings. Ma insisted that she include goddess Ashtabhuja in her ballet. Hema explained that it was too late to incorporate any changes in the production, but Ma persisted and even suggested an appropriate placing for the divine appearance. 'After the abduction of Sita by Ravan, a heartbroken Ram prays to the goddess before his attack on Lanka. That is the place where you can bring goddess Durga,' she suggested. 'And you should enact Durga, no one else.'

Hema was in conflict. She could not decline Ma's request and discussed the possibilities with Bhushan Lakhandri. Together they worked out a situation where Hema changes from Sita costume to the goddess to emerge before Lord Ram. 'It meant costume and choreography alterations, also new movements involving other artistes. The enormity of Ma's message was to dawn on me much later. For some reason Ma wanted goddess Durga to protect me and this was the only way she could assure it.'

They were performing close to ten shows held over weekends and the team was spending a lot of time together. At the end of two months everyone felt bonded and despondent at the thought of parting. 'On our last show at Shrine Auditorium in Los Angeles, I was getting ready in my make-up room, when I sensed a sinking feeling ... I mentioned this to Bhushan. He said he was feeling low too. The disquietude had a reason. As a Hindu I've been reared to believe that the divine visits those with faith. For all these days, it was almost as if the gods and the goddesses were travelling with us through the ballet. And now that our shows were drawing to an end, it was time for the divine to part ways with us too.'

After all these years Hema feels nostalgic about her various dance shows, recalls that in the beginning the invitations for these ballets came from modest organizers settled in remote states who most of the time could not believe that film star Hema Malini had accepted their invitation. But Hema did not let her stardom or ego come in the way of her commitment. Once on stage, she lent the show the same glory and passion that she has lent to her films or to her solo Bharatanatyam dance recital anywhere in the world. There were times when they performed in biting winter and times when they danced in sweltering summer but the hardships were worth it because of the love and the adulation of the people. The audience comprised a simple, slightly overawed crowd but sincere patrons of the art. Hema says those were humbling experiences. 'Everytime I returned from these villages I had learnt something new about life and humanity from my audience. I cherish all those experiences. It was through my interactions with them that our shows evolved and grew.'

Gradually her ballets came to be recognized and in time to come, gained popularity. Natyavihar Kala Kendra was growing and evolving. The productions were becoming bigger and the responsibilities were increasing as well. Jaya Chakravarti, who had all this while been accompanying Hema on her shows, was now getting on in age and found it difficult to cope with Hema's hectic schedule. Quietly, she took a backseat while her older son Kannan stepped into her shoes.

Now Kannan started accompanying Hema on all her dance tours in India and abroad. If Hema's father was recognized as V.S.R. Chakravarti amongst his colleagues, Kannan was recognized as R.K. Chakravarti amongst his professional circle. Like his father, Kannan took over the mantle of presenting Hema's solo and ballet performances. The anchoring involved deep understanding and research on the subject, so Kannan like his appa, began reading relevant literature to include precious minute details in the introduction of the story that made the show all the more memorable. Hema valued and depended on her family's participation in her progress. Whenever she conceived a new ballet or a solo show, she discussed it with her brothers and when the music and the choreography was ready, she invited them along with her sisters-in-law to attend rehearsals and offer

Durga: *The ballet never fails to get a thundering applause from the audience.*

Savitri: *Hema regards this ballet as her superior dances because of the unique interpretation of Lord Yama.*

suggestions. Whenever Hema performed a new show, they were always present in the auditorium lending their support.

There is a story behind how she conceived her next ballet. After playing goddess Ashtabhuja in *Ramayan*, Hema had turned a devotee of goddess Durga to an extent that after her return from the US tour she had begun fasting on Fridays. 'When Ma discovered how deeply affected I was by the goddess, she advised that I was ready to stage an entire ballet on Durga,' shares Hema.

The Hindu scriptures, Vedas and Puranas, describe the worship of the Mother Goddess as an integral part of the *Santana dharma*. The Mother's boundless mercy and compassion for her children have inspired several legendary stories. Universally worshipped as Durga (Mahamaya or Saptasati), this ballet narrates stories of Devi Mahamaya and mirrors multiple incarnations of the mother: Sati, Parvati, Durga and Kali. Of these Durga is the most formidable goddess of the Hindu pantheon and Hema had for a long time been obsessed with her powers.

Legend has it that a bovine demon, Mahishasur conquered the gods and established his power in heaven. The vanquished gods led by Brahma, approached Shiva and Vishnu for advice. Seeing their plight, an enraged Shiva and Vishnu emit fire from which emerged the limb of a woman which slowly transformed into features of several gods: she had the face of Shiva, head of Yama, waist of Indra and shoulders of Vishnu. Looming large and powerful, she multiplied herself into nine images and destroyed the entire army of Mahishasur. 'I had heard this story innumerable times from my mother when I was growing up and remembered every detail very vividly. The demon transforming himself alternately into an elephant and lion … His most ferocious attacks come in his original form as a buffalo … The goddess guzzling supreme liquor and diving into the air ... treading on Mahishasur's throat and piercing him with her spear uncontrollable in her victory … I longed to portray her rampage on stage when Lord Shiva has to prostrate himself as a corpse to stop her madness. It is only when she steps on Shiva's body that she realizes her folly. The image of her tongue hanging out is her acceptance of repentance,' narrates Hema.

Hema says that the dynamism of the goddess enables her to drop all inhibitions on stage. 'When I perform the Kali rampage I'm startled by my own energy and the display is unnerving even for the audience. In fact the production unit is superstitious about my costumes and jewellery worn for the ballet. They believe that it exudes such strong vibrations that it has to be stored in a separate trunk and kept away from the rest of the luggage.'

In the ballet, Bhushan Lakhandri describes Hema's transformation from the *bhikshini* (beggar) to the goddess as surrealistic. 'Even though I have myself choreographed the scene where she is held between two fabrics and emerges as the incarnation, I'm stunned when it happens. Every time she performs that movement I wonder if it is in fact her or the real goddess. That's how powerful she is on stage. The moment has

Mahalakshmi: *Hema associates the goddess with her mother. Jaya painted her while Hema was in her womb.*

never failed to get us a thundering applause from the audience.' *Durga* is Natyavihar Kala Kendras' most popular show and always draws full houses, with lighting in the earlier shows by the renowned Tapas Sen, who till his demise was an integral part of the Natyavihar Kala Kendra family.

According to another legend, Aswapathy, the noble king of Madradesa, was a yogi of high attainment, given to deep contemplation. He propitiates goddess Gayatri so that she will reincarnate as Savitri and resolve the problems of mankind. Trilokanchari Narad Muni with his sixth sense is alerted of Gayatri's divine birth and warns Yama that Savitri will, in time to come, assume enormous powers that will challenge his role as the God of Death. But Yama dismisses Narad.

What attracted Hema to perform the ballet was the character's extraordinary will and determination. Inspired from the book by Sri Aurobindo, Savitri was not merely an extraordinary wife who brings her husband back from the jaws of death, but also an extraordinary person to be able to mislead Lord Yama. Her wisdom and presence of mind will remain an inspiration to a generation of women. Hema reveals that *Savitri* is not amongst her popular ballets because the theme dwells on death. However, she regards it as among her superior dances because of the unique interpretation of Lord Yama. 'Most of us perceive him as an evil incarnation, but our ballet interprets him as a strong and silent god. In fact the actor playing the part has specific instructions to not portray him as evil. For me, it was an added challenge to perform on the elaborate sets. In show business the entire packaging from stagecraft to lighting, costumes to make-up, every little detail is important. If you fail even in one department the effect is not the same,' she remarks.

It was an enlightening phase and unknown to Hema, something deep and profound was churning within her consciousness. For a while it seemed like distant images and echoes she could not define. She wondered if it was her dedication as a dancer, but she sensed shadows of incomplete vision. Flashes appeared and disappeared ... He seemed like the robust, forceful image of Lord Shiva, but Hema was not sure and let the thought pass. Then one day, while she was in Simla for a shooting and in the midst of a conversation with her hairdresser, she was certain that she saw the image again. It was an overpowering image ... and there was no mistaking that the Lord had emerged himself! He was exactly the way Ma had described him – blue body, bright eyes, copper locks left loose and wrapped with malas and trishul – he was divinely exotic and supremely intimidating. For a while Hema wondered if she was hallucinating. Could this be the result of her conversation with her guruma. Hema was perplexed. She turned to look at the image again but it had disappeared. The vision haunted Hema and she discussed the miracle with her guruma later. Ma was not surprised. 'Just flow with it, one does not have to analyse everything.'

Goddess Sri or Mahalakshmi, as she is popularly known is the embodiment of Shakti – the female power – and is also a symbol of prosperity. She is the glorious spouse of Lord Vishnu and the representative of virtues that every woman seeks to emulate. Her throne, the lotus, symbolizes the importance of pure living. The King of the Ocean is overjoyed to receive her and

Radha Krishna: *A ballet of lyrical beauty.*

embraces Lakshmi in his fold. 'The *sagar manthan* where Lakshmi is the last to emerge and captivate both the gods and the demons is my favourite story … I associate this goddess with my mother. Amma painted her while I was in her womb, and my name Hema was derived from the garland Lakshmi wears around her neck. I have grown up looking at the painting where she stands on a lotus. I have performed Lakshmi as a child with chorus dancers. This ballet is a tribute to that childhood memory,' she muses dreamily.

Hema conceived the *Radha Krishna* ballet because she was not content with just enacting the devotee of the Lord. She was now greedy to play his beloved. During the scripting of the ballet, she made several trips to Vrindavan. 'I wandered on the streets … the gardens … saw the grazing cows and imagined the shepherds Krishna played with in his lifetime. I met several ISKCON devotees, heard their fascinating stories and experienced a miracle myself. In the temple lodge I was put up in, there were no luxuries like geysers. Vrindavan is biting cold in the winter and it's impossible to bathe in cold water. I woke up at dawn to attend the *mangala aarti* but could not muster courage to bathe in cold water. As I ran the tap, however, to my amazement I discovered warm water,' she confides eyes sparkling.

In this ballet the choreography attempts to bring to light a few notable events during Lord Krishna's sojourn on earth, particularly his youthful *leela* for which he is venerated. The stage presentation depicts the Lord's mischief with the *gopis* of Vrindavan, the special bond between Radha and Krishna and incidents depicting the Lord using his extraordinary powers to annihilate demon Arishtasur. 'Radha and Krishna are the eternal lovers. I have been performing the various incarnations of Krishna since my childhood. Krishna is alluring because he is the greatest *parakrami*. For more than two decades it has been a tradition for me to perform on the Janmashtami day at the ISKCON fund-raising concerts. Dancing on that day for me is a spiritual experience …

'Something happens to all of us when we perform the *maharaas* in the climax. It is as if an electric energy possesses everybody. It sounds exaggerated but at that moment, I genuinely experience the Lord amidst us. I feel he has descended to dance with all of us and I have a philosophy for this. Imagine 16,000 gopis craved for his attention, but I'm privileged to be in his company. For the audience watching the ballet, it may be just another dance drama. But for me enacting the part, I am Radha incarnate and feel the Lord beside me. That is why when it is time for the *maharaas*, no matter how tired or drained I am, I get a rush of adrenalin. Ravindra Jain's soothing music adds to the sparkle and it is as if I'm transported to Vrindavan mesmerized by the moonlight and the humming bees when Radha and the other *gopis* come alive on stage …

'It has to be some divine power because the most ordinary looking artistes enacting the part of Shiva, Vishnu or Krishna, end up looking godly on stage. It has happened so many times even though the actors performing the Lord have changed from time to time.'

Geet Govind is a poem of lyrical beauty composed by Jayadeva in the twelfth century. It describes the many layers in the extraordinary relationship shared between Radha and Krishna. From their physical attraction to the spiritual bonding, the poem comes a full circle when the Lord accepts Radha into his fold, more as a devotee than as a companion. Hema explains, 'It is intriguing that only Radha is the recipient of Krishna's affection when all the gopis love him equally. I just love this ballet for the sensuality and the erotica between the lovers. Radha is annoyed with Krishna and sulking. To pacify her, Krishna does all she asks him to, applies *chandan* paste on her bust and even sketches intricate designs over her. Unwilling to forgive his betrayal, she full-throatedly expresses her jealousy towards other gopis, scolds him, nags him and bullies him to an extent that he falls at her feet. My friends who are ISKCON devotees get scandalized when they watch the Lord falling at his beloved's feet. They cover their eyes

Dream Girl: Moviegoers missed a heartbeat every time Hema flashed her radiant smile into the camera.

Top: *Hema Malini with Rani Mukherji in a still from* Baabul.

Facing page: Baghbaan – *A dream role about a dream couple ... a role of a lifetime.*

Bottom: *Hema Malini with Amitabh Bachchan in a still from* Baabul.

'There is a side to her personality that is very gregarious and affectionate which she takes great care not to reveal to outsiders.'

Gulzar

Hema Malini with her mother Jaya Chakravarti – As Hema grew older, she discovered that her mother had special dreams for her future.

Whenever Hema thought of a life partner, she always imagined someone like Dharmendra – handsome, strong, with a peaceful face. Hema Malini with Dharmendra.

Top: *'I accept my destiny ... Dharamji and I shared a few good years together and the result is our two beautiful daughters.' Hema Malini, Dharmendra with Esha and Ahana.*

Bottom: *It is just one life and there are so many dreams ... Today, Hema is happy that she faced the challenges that came her way.*

Top: *A woman of her own mind. Hema has explored varied art mediums like films, television, stage, and direction.*

Facing page: *'I want my daughters to persue some form of art ... This can only enrich them.'*

Bottom: *Hema performing with Esha and Ahana .*

The Mother's boundless mercy and compassion for her children, Durga *narrates stories of Devi Mahamaya and mirrors multiple incarnations of the mother.*

' ... dance is not just a passion but a way of life.'

'After innumerable shows of Ramayan *it is almost as if I have been privy to the romance of Ram and Sita.'*

'When I step on the stage in my costume I transform into the character and live with her long after the lights go out.'

Over the years nritya *has helped Hema evolve as a person and a performer.*

Top: *As an evolved Krishna devotee immersed in the* madurya bhav *for her Lord.*

Bottom: *Performing on stage since the age of six ... Hema has grown up surrounded by the sound of applause and the spot light.*

For her valuable contribution in the field of cinema, Hema Malini was awarded the Padmashri in 2000. Receiving the award from President K.R. Narayanan.

Geet Govind: *A path-breaking ballet that delves into the sensuality and erotica between Radha and Krishna.*

in embarrassment because they cannot see their Lord thus! But Radha is stubborn and demanding, and Krishna indulges her by oiling her hair and tying it in braids, applying kajal to her eyes and dons her with jewels.'

Hema describes *Geet Govind* as a path-breaking ballet unacceptable to staunch Krishna devotees. Her reason why the ballet is not as popular as others is because the lyrics are in Sanskrit. 'It is really sad that the oldest language of our country is not comprehended by the majority of the people. But this does not discourage our team. We have performed too many shows to mistake popular ratings for merit,' emphasizes Hema. Deepak Mazumdar, choreographer of *Geet Govind* adds that to the four vedas created by Lord Brahma in our Upanishads, Bharat Muni added a fifth veda – *Natyashastra* – because it included *gyan* (enlightenment), *shilpa* (sculpture), *kala* (art), *vidya* (knowledge), *yoga* (science of discipline) and *karma* (deeds). No wonder, dance

Draupadi: *A fascinating tale of intrigue, machinations, quarrels and sacrifice, this ballet tells the story from Draupadi's point of view.*

gurus relate the art form to the language of the divine. In fact Mazumdar believes that artistes are angels of the Almighty sent to earth for a bigger purpose and that is why they are untouched by age and undiminished in charisma. Associated with Natyavihar Kala Kendra for more than two decades, Mazumdar describes Hema's passion for dance as a spiritual journey and her various ballets an endeavour to uplift the audiences and re-acquaint them with ancient scriptures. Hema on her part credits her entire team for their success. 'I'm fortunate to have such a marvellous group

continuing with me for so many years from one ballet to another,' she acknowledges in all humility.

The rich tapestry of the *Mahabharata* lends itself to a myriad interpretations. Hema always wanted to perform a ballet on Draupadi but was never completely satisfied with the interpretation in scripts offered to her. Then one day, while browsing in a bookshop, Hema came across renowned Oriya writer Pratibha Ray's novel *Yajnaseni*. 'I read the novel the same night, talked to the author and set up a meeting. Out of all the women I have portrayed in my ballets, I feel most compassionate towards Draupadi. The pain and humiliation Draupadi endured nobody else did. Imagine a woman sharing five brothers as husbands, being publicly disrobed and finally abandoned at the Kailash Parbat. Despite five husbands, in her moment of crisis it is her mentor and friend Krishna who comes to her rescue,' Hema reflects.

A tapestry of fascinating tales of intrigue, machinations, quarrels and sacrifice, the ballet tells the story from Draupadi's point of view. It is Natyavihar Kala Kendra's most expensive production so far, combining for the first time the two mediums of audio-visual and performance. The ballet has more drama than dance and therefore for the first time television artistes were cast in the role of Pandavas and Kauravas. Bhushan Lakhandri was responsible for their performances and choreography. 'We researched on the subject for almost a year before we went on stage. It was the longest we have worked on any of our productions. All our other productions were conceived and choreographed within a year,' informs Hema.

Parampara signifies the tradition of passing knowledge from one generation to another. A dance ballet is the choreography of an original composition comprising Bharatanatyam and Odissi dance forms, the former performed by Hema Malini and the latter by her daughters, Esha and Ahana Deol. The presentation is a pragmatic acceptance of fusion dance forms, appropriately projected by two generations of dancers. 'My mother gifted me the art and I have passed on the legacy to my daughters,' smiles Hema. 'Words can't describe the experience of performing on stage with my daughters. We have performed shows everywhere in the world, including at the Tirupati temple recently, and the feeling of performing in a divine place is absolutely sublime.'

Hema is often asked why she only opts for mythological figures for her ballets. Her explanation is that how can classical dance deviate from the gods and the temples when the

Parampara: *The tradition of passing knowledge from one generation to another. Hema with her daughters Esha and Ahana.*

Natyashastra is steeped in mythology. That Hema has a traditional demeanour and is naturally inclined to spirituality adds magic to her regal presence on stage. Those who have seen the live performances say that Hema is so mesmerizing that she transports the audience to a different world and experience.

Her recent addition *Yashoda Krishna* is a tribute to universal motherhood. Yashoda was not Krishna's biological mother but she loved him to a point of obsession. Krishna was the life of Vrindavan and the joy of all the gopis. He harassed them, purloined their garments and when they complained to Yashoda, he pleaded innocent. The ballet elaborates on Krishna's leela … his pranks and miracles. 'Krishna appears in all my ballets because he creates an impact in all the roles he plays – as a son, friend and lover. *Yashoda Krishna* is slightly different from my other ballets in the sense it is based on folklore and designed for a wider audience,' she explains.

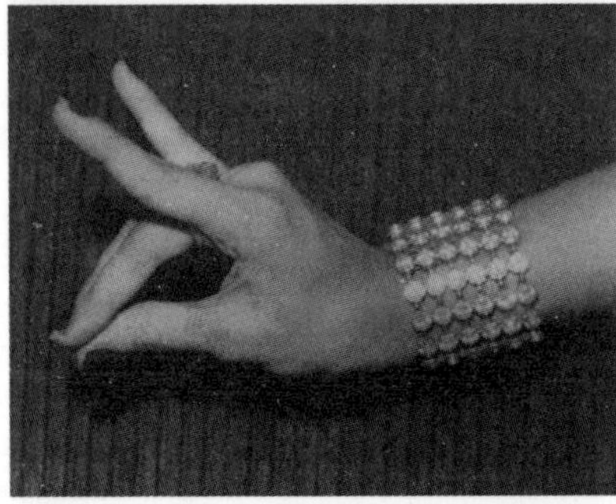

Hema demonstrating several mudras.

Hema says that this is her first experience of working with a child on stage, 'It calls for special skill to work with child artistes. On stage it is even more difficult, for one is never sure which corner of the stage the infant will begin crawling!' The ballet depicts various stages of Krishna's childhood and Ahana performs the final twelve-year-old, 'My favourite items of hers are the *Kaalia Mardan* and the *Govardhan*. In both, Ahana is so effective that everyone always comments on her alluring quality,' says the proud mother.

Hema reveals that Kavita Krishnamurthy has rendered all the songs of her ballets, 'Kavita is my mother's discovery and I have immense faith in her voice. Just in the way Lata Mangeshkar is my voice in films, Kavita is my voice on stage.'

Bhushan Lakhandri, who has been associated with Hema's banner for over a decade, and has choreographed all her ballets beginning with *Nritya Mallika* and *Meera* right upto *Yashoda Krishna* and *Draupadi.* Only *Geet Govind* and *Parampara,* are pure classicals and are choreographed by Hema's colleague Deepak Mazumdar. Lakhandri says it has been an enriching association with Hema Malini. He adds that it is not easy to sustain a creative relationship for such a long duration without conflicts. 'We were able to do so because Hema does not impose herself as a producer. She has been dancing for more than three decades but even now she is as enthusiastic as a newcomer. When the telephone in my house shrills at 7 a.m., everyone knows that it can only be Hemaji. She is an early riser and the wake-up call usually means that she wants to share a brainwave. The last time she woke me up was to tell me that she wanted to include a pure Kathak item in her ballet *Draupadi.* What's more interesting is that she had even thought of the place where the item ought to be incorporated. Her enthusiasm and energy for her art is simply amazing. With her position and stature, she can so easily turn complacent, but she is all the time on the move … '

After so many years, Bhushan still remembers their first performance together on stage. Minutes before the curtain went up, she turned to ask him if her *mudras* were right, 'I could not believe it … Despite so much success there is still a child-like quality about her. After all these years, before the show she is all the time revising her steps … And that is how she has trained her daughters too.'

Roots and Shadows

Esha and Ahana Deol grew up with the sound of music around them. As little girls they have memories of a very motivated mother matching her steps to song renditions. Their home would be filled with musicians and dancers. Rehearsals began for all of them early in the morning and stretched till late evening. In those days, Esha tried every trick in the book to bunk school and sometimes Hema would relent. Esha looked forward to occasions when she could sit in a corner with a notebook in hand, jotting down each time a dancer missed a step.

'I knew all the steps and songs by heart, and often joined the dancers unnoticed,' recalls Esha. 'I distracted the dancers from rehearsals, but no matter how much of a racket I created, I was never stopped from being a part of the rehearsals.' Esha feels this instilled a lot of confidence in her. 'As a baby, I fell ill every time Mama went out of town. Later, when I could accompany her during her shootings, the anxieties settled down,' she elucidates. During her vacations, Esha was a permanent fixture at her mother's shootings. Hema's make-up dada, to keep her occupied,

Facing Page: *'My mother gifted me the art and I have passed on the legacy to my daughters.' Hema with Esha and Ahana.*

would paint her face and spread Hema's duppatta on her pretty head while papa Dharmendra's loud voice ... 'No films for you Esha,' boomed in her head.

Esha played truant in school, so Hema hired a private tutor to ensure that she completed her homework. The tutor taught her all the subjects except history because Hema enjoyed teaching her the subject and Esha scored good marks in it. 'Mama would sit with a foot-ruler revising my history homework with me. How I hated her those days. Today, I find her effort so overwhelming. She could have so easily left it to the tutor but she preferred to do it herself,' Esha says looking back.

Younger daughter Ahana remembers playing in the garden where Hema and her troupe would be rehearsing the ballet. Her cousin Prabha would distract her with little scraps of paper to scribble upon. When Ahana got tired of scrawling, she would play with any dancer who was free to shower attention on her.

Both the sisters have vivid memories of Hema's green room on the eve of the show. They would gaze at their mother in amazement while she got ready in front of an enormous mirror. Esha would play with her make-up tray, touching the pinks and the blues, fascinated with the wonders the colours could do to a human face. On festivals, Hema entertained her daughters by painting their faces and dressing them up in elaborate costumes, usually improvised with accessories from her wardrobe. On Janmashtami, Esha would be dressed as Krishna, complete with peacock feathers, while Ahana would be Balram in a dhoti! Like her mother, Esha stepped on stage for the first time when she was six years old. Hema was staging her new ballet *Meera.* A dialogue, '*Jab Meera saat saal ki thi* ...' justified Esha's presence on stage. She loved being dressed in a vibrant ghaagra choli and being fussed over. She particularly enjoyed the curtain call when her name was announced and she had to come forward and take a bow. And of course at the end of the show, stand in a queue with the rest of the artistes to collect her remuneration of Rs 200! 'I was never allowed to spend this money. Neither has Mama touched it in all

There is nothing as rewarding and fulfilling as seeing your children grow: Hema's two precious daughters, Esha and Ahana.

these years. I am sure those currency notes are still carefully wrapped within the folds of her innumerable saris,' smiles Esha.

Esha and Ahana say that the enormity of performing on stage never dawned on them until much later. Perhaps because Hema treated it so naturally. When Hema was staging *Ramayan*, she enrolled them as part of Lord Ram's vanarsena as baby monkeys, who help Lord Ram cross the sea, and later as baby monsters in Ravan's court! One of the servant boys at home had taught Esha to do cartwheels and she pestered Hema to include the step as a part of the choreography. It was a moment the girls enjoyed thoroughly. In the following ballet *Durga*, they made sedate appearances as incarnations of the Nav Durga.

They were accustomed to having a working mother but did not really know how many different things she juggled at the same time. All that mattered to them was that their mother was present when they needed her. Their best family moments were during dinner-time, watching television together. Hema would recount stories about her childhood, tell them how she resented dancing as a little girl and how their grandmother (whom the girls addressed as Amba) never allowed her to lose focus. Snuggled close to her on the wide bed they would ask for more stories. Hema never read them the conventional fairy tales. Instead, she narrated them stories from mythology. Not surprising that Esha and Ahana followed all her ballets – *Ramayan, Meera* and *Durga* – and needed no explanations.

As Esha entered her teens her life opened up to a host of new interests, particularly football. She and her classmates would spend eight hours of the day on the playground kicking the football, much to the consternation of her parents. Irrespective of their other distractions it was difficult for Esha and Ahana to escape dance rehearsals. Music reverberated through the house at all times as Hema went about her daily chores and Esha and Ahana unknowingly hummed along, doing their homework. One summer vacation Esha and her school friends participated in a folk dance competition held at the Brabourne Stadium but it was more for the fun of wearing *Koli* saris and tying their hair in a bun decorated with flowers. As she grew older, Esha felt the pressure from her mother to start learning dance and she began to resent it. Wherever she went and whoever she met, the conversation invariably drifted to the crucial question. Strangers she had never met asked, 'So are you learning dance as well?' There would be an awkward silence while Hema made some lame excuse and Esha rolled her eyes and looked away. This continued for some time. Ahana recalls that she was six years old when she began her formal training in dance. 'Esha and I travelled thrice a week to a dance school in Khar. Our first guruji, Deepak Mazumdar was a qualified teacher but not worthy of truant students like us. We were interested in dance but were not focussed enough to pursue it sincerely,' confesses Ahana.

Being a perfectionist Mazumdar would make the girls go over the same *adavus* until they had mastered the footwork, but the monotony of routine frustrated the girls and the lessons failed to retain their interest. Hema understood the problem and despite stiff opposition from her daughters, kept up her efforts. After less than a year of training under Mazumdar, Hema arranged for another master from the famous dance school Kala Sadan in Matunga to come home and teach them. And to make sure that they remained focussed, she included their friend Faza in the group. If the guru fell ill or was travelling, Hema would promptly find a replacement. Not only that, she enrolled them in additional workshops she thought worth attending.

During this time Hema was training in Odissi from Guru Rabindra Atibudhi for a special item to be incorporated in her ballet. Since it was school vacation time, Hema thought it would be a good idea to include her daughters in the lessons as well. This time she requested the tutor to refrain from repetitive lessons. Atibudhi had the rare art of adapting to his shishyas' temperament. He sensed they were restless and dealt with them very gently. Instead of pushing them to perfection he made the lessons seem like recreation, taught them new steps and *mudras* and then left them to explore themselves. Hema watched their progress, amazed at Atibudhi's mastery and triumph. The strategy was working wonders. This was the first time when Esha and Ahana looked forward to their dance classes.

Esha's obsession with football continued and she would escape to the playground whenever she got the opportunity. Hema disapproved of the sport and looked upon it as an invasion into dance, but avoided any sort of confrontation with her daughter. Esha says that she had never anticipated that a day would come when she would have to choose between football and something else, but it did. She was in the final term of her ninth standard and selected to represent her school at an inter-school sports event in Chandigarh. But her father put his foot down. Dharmendra disapproved of the idea of his daughter wearing shorts and

Esha at Osho Ashram – in one of her earliest solo performances.

running on the field kicking a ball. Had Gurinder Chadha's *Bend It Like Beckham* released a few years earlier, probably it could have changed the course of Esha's destiny. But at that point, football was taboo in the family. Esha says that she took to dance more out of vengeance. 'Football had left an aching vacuum in my life and I was trying to compensate that loss,' she reflects.

One sunny afternoon, Esha was at home, watching an Odissi performance on television with her grandmother and something clicked. She decided, on the spur of the moment, that she would pursue Odissi instead of Bharatanatyam. She shared her thoughts with Amba and later with Hema. Hema was a trifle disappointed but Esha explained to her that she did not want to pursue a dance where she was uncomfortable with the posture. 'Bharatanatyam left me with aching knees. Odissi, in comparison, has fluid movements and even the postures are not as strenuous,' she justifies her choice. Hema relented reluctantly. It was Jaya Chakravarti who convinced Hema that as long as Esha pursued any classical form of dance it did not matter whether she learnt Bharatanatyam or Odissi.

Her first dance recital was at the ISKCON Auditorium in Mumbai, for Guru Ravindra Atibudhi's annual function. Eight students were selected from different batches of the dance academy to perform *Dasawtar.* Esha played the main part of Vishnu. The following day, an eveninger published Esha's photograph. This inspired the Nehru Centre faculty to contact Hema for a solo concert by Esha for their annual Rimjhim Festival. Hema was flattered by the proposal but knew that Esha was not yet ready for it. The faculty persisted nevertheless. Hema did not want to miss the opportunity. She discussed the possibilities with Esha's guru, Atibudhi. He sensed the urgency and took it up as a challenge to prepare Esha for the recital – the guru-shishya worked as though possessed.

Within two months they were ready for the show. This was an unprecedented feat! Esha cannot forget the heady feeling she woke up with that morning … or the funny feeling in the pit of her stomach as they drove to the Nehru Auditorium in Worli, Mumbai. 'I can never forget Mama's face ... She was a nervous wreck but tried not to show it. She stood in the wings clutching at the curtain, watching my every step,' recalls Esha.

There was a reason for this. The previous evening Hema had booked the ISKCON Auditorium to supervise Esha's dress rehearsal. She wanted to make sure that Esha understood the importance of centre stage. She drew circles to mark out the inner and outer space of her position. Esha absorbed all her instructions carefully. When it was time to start the rehearsal, Esha froze. Seeing her mother sit in the first row of the large auditorium, Esha could not meet her gaze. 'She said she would not perform if I was in the auditorium. It was an absurd condition but I did not want to argue and add to her tension, so I came backstage and we began her dance recital,' sighs Hema.

Esha delivered a flawless performance that day. Not only did Hema stay out of Esha's orbit, but also backstage, Hema made sure to position herself in a manner that she would not make eye contact with her. Mother and daughter have come a long way since then.

Three years later, Ahana performed her solo recital at the same venue and for the same occasion. Hema looked upon it as the continuity of a tradition. Ahana reveals that she wanted to learn dance only because she liked watching her mother. 'She is so graceful. You watch her walk, stand or sit and you know immediately that she is a dancer. Her shoulders are always upright, tummy tucked in and feet folded. On stage she glides like a swan. Esha and I watch her perform a *mudra* and try enacting it, but somehow the effect is never the same. You give her any pose and she carries it off so well.'

When the sisters were preparing for their first show together, Hema warned them that there would be comparisons with her, but that should not deter them. Says Ahana, 'It is not fair to compare Esha and me with Mama. We cannot be like her. I cannot perform the way she does. I have to evolve a style of my own. But it's a cross that all celebrity children must bear. While we will always have a set of genuine friends who will ride with us through our bad times, there will be another group, seeking our friendship for the obvious reasons. It's not always easy to recognize their motives. The process is long and often confusing. But one has to gamble.'

When they were younger, and Hema described her experience on stage as spiritual, her daughters could not relate to her feelings. But today, they do. 'Something churns inside me everytime I make an entry on stage,' says Esha. 'When I perform the introductory *mangala charan* in praise of Lord Jagannath and I hear the interlude music, I get very emotional sometimes to the extent that I start crying. It takes a lot of effort to hold myself back. I have discussed this with Mama and she assures me that the anxieties would subside with time,' Esha ponders.

Esha often wonders how her mother went through the various phases of her life without ever letting her emotions get the better of her. 'She neither had the freedom nor close friends like us. She had no social contacts except for the family. I don't know how she contained herself. As children we have arbitrarily invaded her creative space ... I have phoned her with inconsequential matters like asking for a compass-box just ten minutes before she made her entry on stage. I feel so ashamed of it now. How could we have been so cruel? It is amazing how her sheer presence instils so much faith. Today, I know that Mama can get me out of any problem, provided I don't betray her confidence. She has to just hear my voice and know how I'm feeling. After learning to dance and being on stage myself, I appreciate her all the more. She is special because she is not just my mama but also my guru . . .' she emphasizes.

Esha describes her relationship with her father as more formal and adds that she was always in awe of her papa. 'After so many years, even now when I'm talking to him over the phone, I stand in attention . . . But despite the fear, there are no deprivations. Papa was always around when we needed him. May be we saw him lesser but he was always there ... For Ahana and my birthdays, during summer vacation when we went out on holidays,' she recalls as wave of nostalgia sweeps over her. Esha and Ahana have amusing memories of their holiday in Paris as children. Once at the Geneva Airport, Dharmendra, unaccustomed to travelling without assistance, went from one gate to another because he could not locate the exit. 'While Papa was getting flustered, Ahana and I could not stop laughing because we could not believe that grown ups can lose their way too,' chuckles Esha. Another funny episode on the same trip was when they were travelling by an early morning train from Geneva to Oslo. 'Papa was so nervous about missing the train that in his anxiousness he made us board the earlier train. We realized this when we arrived at our destination much before schedule. We still laugh over it after all these years.'

Ahana reveals that her most hilarious moment with her father was when the two got lost while shopping at Harrods in London. 'Somehow we got separated from Mama, and Papa could not locate her. I don't know how we landed at the Lost-and-Found counter where they announced my name over the loudspeaker and Mama came looking out for me. Not in her wildest imagination had she expected that in a corner, holding my hand would be an equally scared Papa.'

Both aver that they never visited their father on the sets and say accompanying Mama was far more exciting because 'though Mama was very disciplined we always had our way with her,' they reveal with a naughty look in their eyes.

Esha states that her natural confidence stems from her school, Jamnabai Narsee. She says the school has been the strongest influence in her formative years, 'This school prepares you to go a long way in life. You can always tell a Jamnabai student in a crowd. It's the only institution I know that makes no discrimination amongst students.' This was not so when she joined the Mithibai College in Vile Parle. 'They never let me forget that I was Dharmendra and Hema Malini's daughter. From the moment I

Dharmendra's loud voice ... 'No films for you Esha' boomed in her head.

entered the gate I heard murmurings of "Esha Deol ... " everywhere. It was so annoying! I hated going to college and after one miserable year I preferred to opt out and appear privately for the exams. It made me realize that unless you are happy with what you do, you cannot prosper.'

She dropped out of college in the second year and that was the time film producers started wooing her with proposals to act in films. For a long time Hema did not tell her about the offers. Then one day, a little shyly, Hema asked Esha if she was interested in working in films. Without a moment's hesitation, Esha nodded vigorously. She had always wanted to be an actress but had not expressed it out of fear of her father. It was not easy to convince Dharmendra but the combined efforts of Ahana and Hema broke his defences and finally Dharmendra relented but with a lot of preconditions. He was worried about her playing ultra modern roles or shooting in unsafe locations. He warned Esha to stay away from negative publicity and conduct herself with the same dignity as her mother.

Parampara : Passing knowledge from one generation to another.

Esha was eighteen when she made her debut in Boney Kapoor's Vinay Shukla-directed *Koi Mere Dil Se Pooche* and later *Na Tum Jaano Na Hum*. In the coming years she signed more films like *Kya Dil Ne Kaha, Chura Liya Hain Tumne, LOC Kargil, Yuva, Dhoom, Kaal* and several others. No matter how busy Esha became with her film career, like her mother, she always remained committed to dance. 'Mama was my inspiration and I wanted to mould my career on her.' Esha reveals that when younger, she watched, 'only her lighthearted movies like *Seeta Aur Geeta*. But after I became an actress, I watched her other films like *Khushboo* as well, and was amazed at her range. She was as convincing as a princess as a pauper. She rode bikes and was also portrayed as the damsel in distress. She had the rare quality of looking compatible with all her co-stars be it Dev Anand, Rajesh Khanna or Amitabh Bachchan. Her best co-star of course was always Papa. Together they were simply magical!' she says.

Esha admits that her mother is her role model. On one hand Esha continues to play the glamour girl in mainstream movies, on the other her commitment to classical dance remains irrevocable. In fact the trio (Hema, Esha and Ahana) stage frequent shows of *Parampara* all over India and abroad. They have held successful shows in Bangkok, Dubai, Hongkong and the US. Some special dates are customarily marked out in their calendar for Natyavihar Kala Kendra, like Janmashtami day for the ISKCON where the trio some years ago, fulfiled Hema's long-time dream of performing *Krishna Balram* with Esha playing Krishna, Ahana playing Balram and Hema playing Yashoda. The other reserved date, 25 June is for *Jaya Smriti* – a tribute to Jaya Chakravarti on her death anniversary – is a unique programme to promote young talent in classical dance.

For outside sponsors prior to confirming a concert, Hema first checks out if the dates suit Esha and Ahana's schedule. Next, she charts out a rigid timetable for rehearsals. Initially they start with a thrice-weekly practise. Later, as the final date draws closer,

Hema extends the duration to build up better stamina. When the show is only a week away, their guruji starts visiting home twice a day. The morning practise is at dawn and waking up is a problem for both the girls, but Hema makes sure they do. In the evenings, Hema insists they watch their old dance recordings to avoid their previous errors. 'This is a little uncomfortable, but we have to do what she says,' smiles Ahana.

On the day of the show, they always prefer to do their make-up at home. It takes approximately two and a half hours for the three of them to be ready. They travel in one car, amidst casual chatter and music. Hema never forgets to enquire if the girls remember their steps, and sometimes does a quick replay of hand movements in chronological order. She always carries the audio CD of the dance recital to listen to during the drive but if the girls are reluctant, she does not impose upon them. At the auditorium they share one room. The adjoining room is reserved for the luggage and for costume change. An ice bucket filled with Glucon bags is compulsory in the room. She makes sure that all of them drink plenty of Electrol. She prefers not to eat a full meal before a dance and that is how she has trained her daughters. However, if they feel like having a pizza, she relents as long as they don't overstuff themselves.

'Once on stage, she treats us like professionals,' says Ahana. 'She does not override our space. If I do a step in a different manner, miss a beat or make a mistake, her face does not register the lapse. She will not even mention it during the interval. It's only when the show is over and we are driving home, that she will pull us up. Very seldom, can I catch her missing a step, but I'm not as generous. I would make it evident right there on stage that I have caught her … She has taught me that when I feel nervous I must think of God and He will give me strength. She says it is not necessary to always make eye contact with the audience. If I look at my hands and execute my steps it looks very graceful. Her golden rule is that I must dance because I enjoy dancing and I follow the good advice,' Ahana admits.

When the show ends, the girls are impatient to get back home. They start removing their jewellery on the way to the green room and throw off their costumes to rush to the waiting car. Hema takes longer on stage because she has to give a thanksgiving speech at the end of the show. The formalities take a while so Hema follows in the second car. 'By the time she is home it is usually late but she never fails to drop by in our rooms and check if we have had our vitamins before we fall asleep,' relates Ahana.

Recently, three of them performed together in Dubai. On a free day they went shopping but were browsing in various departmental stores. This was quite a contrast from the old days when Hema, Ahana and Esha would walk through the same mall and Hema shopped for all of them. 'Those days Ahana and I fought all the time to sit beside Mama which was resolved with her sitting between us. That is how we used to travel everywhere on flights,' smiles Esha. 'Today, of course, when we are travelling together, Mama sleeps in a corner while Esha and I talk amongst ourselves,' laughs Ahana.

Coming Full Circle

It is a crowded lobby outside Fame Adlabs Theatre, Mumbai. It is the star-studded premier of *Main Aisa Hi Hoon*. An excited crowd waits for their favourite stars to arrive at the auditorium. As a blue Mercedes draws up and a ravishing Hema Malini accompanying her daughter Esha Deol alights from the vehicle, there is pandemonium all around. Bodyguards rush to shield the two dazzling ladies on either side and gently usher them to the cordoned zone, but the madness does not subside. The camera lights and the electronic media follow them.

Away from the cacophony, inside the auditorium, Hema recalls her own film premieres over the years. She has lost count of the silver and golden jubilee celebrations she attended with her family in her long career. Her mother was always by her side on these occasions. For years, even the saris Hema wore at these big functions would be hand-picked by Jaya Chakravarti. 'Those days stars wore their personal clothes at functions and parties. Today of course trends have changed and also temperaments. In my time, it was unthinkable for us to go anywhere unescorted. Today, Esha goes everywhere with her friends. If I accompany her, it is

Facing Page: *'My experiences have helped me evolve as a person and an artiste.' Hema with Amitabh Bachchan in a still from* Baghbaan.

only because I want to be a part of the special landmark moments of her career,' explains Hema.

She adds that while technology has opened new vistas in all mediums, it has taken away the simple joys of life. 'In my childhood years, I was not exposed to air-conditioners or even refrigerators till I joined films. In fact the only luxury we possessed was a big radio that was the focal point of the entire family. And yet there were no deprivations,' she reflects.

She adds that her generation had other distinct advantages that are often missing today. For instance, she attributes a major part of her success to the support system provided by her family. 'I was able to spread my wings and dedicate myself wholeheartedly to my career because I was spared of the daily tensions of stardom. I never got into date hassles with any of my producers and there were no heartburns about payments because my fees automatically matched my successes. Similarly, I did not encounter any problems with my staff because if they wanted something they would speak to Amma or Aunty. My family did all they could to raise my comfort zone at my shootings and my dance recitals,' she acknowledges today.

It is due to the long and satisfactory years spent before the arc lights and on stage that Hema is able to define her creative platform through dance shows today. 'I enjoy the entire process – rehearsals, costume trials, the gnawing feeling of anticipation prior to a show, and the elation after the applause, the anxiety of performing before a new audience each time, the joy of sharing the platform with my daughters ... The pride when they are appreciated ... And the rage I feel when they falter ...

'Years ago, when I was a busy star and had little time for dance practise, my mother would send my dance teacher wherever I was shooting in Manali or Madras, and he would make sure that I brush up my lessons after pack-up. I dare not do that with Esha for she will not like it. This is the difference between our generations. We were trained to surrender, while they are reared to negotiate. As parents one cannot interfere beyond a point. I am fortunate that both my daughters are interested in dance. On the day of our show, Esha knows that wherever she is, she has to fly back home. It is easier to make programmes with Ahana because she is rooted in one place, and is able to give more time and concentration.'

Hema says that her daughters have come a long way from their first performance as baby monsters in her ballet *Ramayan*. 'They have progressed in terms of confidence and poise. Ahana is currently playing Krishna in Natyavihar Kala Kendras' new ballet *Yashoda Krishna,* and the transformation in her is amazing. I don't need to remind her about rehearsals or costume trials. She is focused, so is Esha whether she is performing a jazzy number in *Dhoom* or dancing *mangala charan* on stage. Recently the three of us were performing at the Tirupati temple for the *Ugadi* (New Year) celebrations. This was our first experience of performing at a place of worship and it was beyond description. I'm so overwhelmed by the experience that I'm contemplating my new ballet on the glories of Lord Balaji. It's heartening for me as a mother to watch my little girls flourish and become responsible. It's intriguing how life is coming a full circle now. When I was young, my mother looked after me. Later, the roles in the relationship reversed, my mother was the one who needed looking after, just in the way I do now when I am with my girls today,' she remarks thoughtfully.

Looking back, Hema appreciates her mother's ability to keep her firmly rooted to the ground. Otherwise with the kind of celebrity status she enjoyed at such a young age, the flattery could have gone to her head. Hema treasures the experience of being a mother herself. 'Amma struck a balance between praise and criticism without her ever denting my self-confidence … I'm not sure if I'm as good as her in rearing my daughters … I try wholeheartedly. There was a different magic to the older generation. They did not have adequate opportunities or education, but they achieved so much more than we did,' she surmises.

It saddens Hema that someone as dynamic as her mother was repeatedly referred to as 'Hema Malini's mother' by the media. 'It is disgraceful and undermining for an individual. Why do we need to drag a relationship to introduce a person? This only happens in India and more so with film personalities. Or perhaps it's a natural progression and I must learn to accept it without any cynicism. I was referred to as Jaya Chakravarti's daughter when I was a child and a time will soon come when people will address me as Esha and Ahana Deol's mother. It's the proverbial middle-generation syndrome I guess …

'It sounds unbelievable but I used to sleep in my mother's room till I turned thirteen. But special rooms were made for my daughters when they were brought home from the hospital … In school I would not talk to people outside the family while Esha and Ahana are not awed by anyone. My inhibitions came in the way when I began working in films. I would feel awkward sitting opposite strangers narrating scripts to me. Writers expected my participation and I was not willing to give any reactions. On the sets, when the director explained a scene to me, I would insist that my mother sit beside me. Film magazines poked fun at the family for never leaving me alone but the truth was, I was terrified of being on my own, terrified of making mistakes. Only later did I realize that everyone makes mistakes … ,' she admits candidly.

Today as a Member of Parliament who frequently visits the capital, Hema often finds herself searching for that little girl she left behind in the familiar lanes of their old abode. It's been over four decades now but Hema can still recall her sense of wonderment and isolation. 'I was so withdrawn, almost living in my fantasy as a child. Our house had a beautiful painting sketched by Amma – of baby Krishna playing in Vrindavan. We still have that painting in our home in Chennai. This painting for some strange reason always gave me great solace. Every time I was confused or frightened, I imagined myself being Krishna's playmate in Vrindavan … It was a restless phase. There was no reason to, but I felt anxious … Time has abated all those fears. Today, when I'm more reassured, I want to hold the little girl's hand and protect her. I want to tell her "don't be afraid … you had to endure all you did, because I had to emerge from you … "

'Through my various characters on screen, I have led so many lives. I have donned the crown of a princess, known the abandon of a pickpocket. I have stayed inside a mud house of a remote village and walked through the corridors of a palace in my flowing ghaagras. Only artistes are privileged to have such diverse experiences. Through my various dance ballets, I have further discovered other sterling characters. I have sensed the loneliness of Meera trapped inside King Rana's manor, craving for Krishna … I have experienced the sacrifice of Sita going through the trial by fire … After innumerable shows of *Ramayan* it is almost as if I've been privy to the romance of Ram and Sita. Absurd as it may sound, when I'm enacting Sita on stage, I hear echoes of what Ram could have whispered to his beloved …

'Recently when I returned from a one-month trip to the US after performing several shows of *Draupadi,* I fell mysteriously ill. The doctor could not diagnose the ailment but I felt a hollow feeling in my stomach all the time. It was only later that I understood that my illness was the hangover of the trauma of Draupadi. Performing ten shows in ten different cities was like reliving her pain and betrayal. To go through just the enactment of the disrobing on stage is a disturbing experience. I don't know how Draupadi endured it in real life.'

Hema believes that there is no dearth of stimulation in an artiste's life but the euphoria comes with a penalty. The excitement brings along with it innumerable and unforeseen pressures. And nobody can help you ride out this turbulence. Still, the enchantment is worth it. Opportunity knocks on your door once and your fortune is in recognizing those chances.

It is just one life and there are so many dreams. Today, Hema Malini is happy that she faced the challenges that came her way – editorship of a woman's magazine, *New Woman/Meri Saheli* or taking up the post of NFDC chairperson. It is said that the initiative to export Indian cinema in the traditional as well as the non-traditional market was established in her tenure. 'Every time I returned from my various international festivals, I had lucrative suggestions to improve India's visibility in global cinema,' says Hema. The NFDC credits her with significant changes in their scripting committee as well as the production budgets.

Hema campaigned for her co-star and Bharatiya Janata Party candidate, Vinod Khanna in the 1999 general elections. That was the beginning of her political sojourn where large crowds gathered to see the star. Until then, Hema did not nurse any serious ambitions of joining politics. But with Vinod Khanna's campaign proving a huge success, the BJP approached her to campaign in other states as well. Hema travelled to remote villages and everywhere, the response was euphoric. She was herself surprised by the interest she generated. 'There comes a time in an artiste's life when she begins to disbelieve her own popularity but the audience restores her faith back in her and reintroduces her to her own charisma. It was a while that my films were released in theatres. I had kind of got used to a quiet existence. But in my new surroundings, I discovered a new voice and a new platform. As the public cheered me, I felt exhilarated,' she says.

Hema states that she extended her support to the BJP because she believes in the party's ideology. The party had high expectations of her and recommended her strongly. She was on her way to the US for staging her ballet *Radha Krishna*, when she learnt that she was nominated as a Rajya Sabha member, 'There was a buzz that my name was circulating but the confirmation came just when I was boarding the flight. When I stopped at Paris en route, I was flooded with congratulatory messages on my cellphone.'

It was in the winter session of 2003 that the actress was sworn into the Rajya Sabha. She was asked to block a couple of dates when the swearing-in ceremony would be held. One of the dates was 16 October. When Hema discussed her schedule with her mother, Jaya promptly said it should be the 16th. On this date the family held a puja at home every year to seek blessings on Hema's birthday. Not to break the tradition, Jaya Chakravarti organized

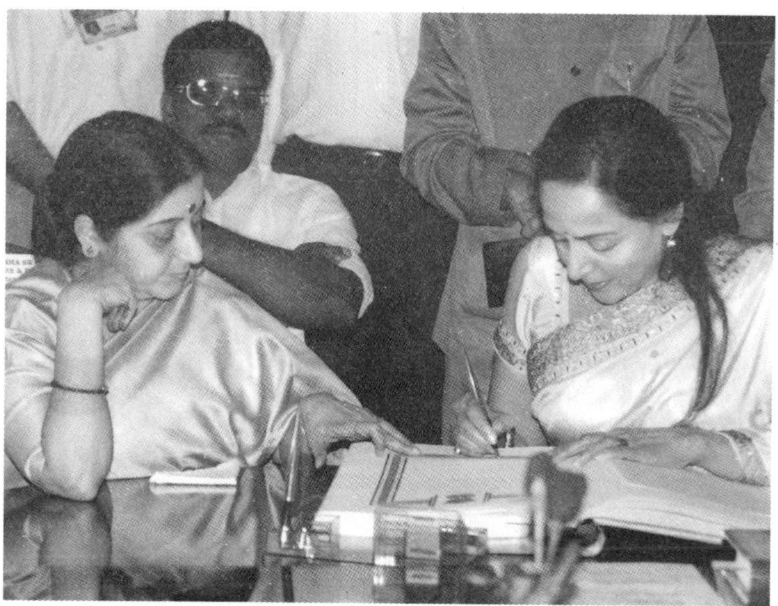

'Politics is a different world altogether.' Hema joined BJP in 2000. Seen here with a BJP stalwart Sushma Swaraj.

an early morning puja to allow her to take the morning flight to Delhi. Unfortunately, the flight got delayed and by the time Hema reached Parliament, the oath ceremony had already begun. Hema was embarrassed to make a late entry but covered up her nervousness by quickly taking the paper and start reading.

In her maiden speech in Parliament, she said, 'I hail from the film world ... a world of dreams and one day, I would like to see these dreams transformed into reality.' She emphasized the need for a film museum in Mumbai on the lines of the Universal Studios in Hollywood. She urged the government to support the project by allotting land and funds. The actress had started as an unlikely candidate but she was learning quickly even though at times she fumbled.

She created a stir as the Rajya Sabha-appointed candidate when, she joined the BJP. It was against the rules for an appointed candidate to join a political party. But since this occurred six

Hema participating in a cleanliness drive with school children in Andheri at Mumbai.

months after her nomination to the Rajya Sabha and considered legitimate according to the party regulations, the controversy was cleared. In 2004, she campaigned for the Lok Sabha elections. 'We travelled in the interiors, places I had never seen or heard about. But wherever we went, large crowds awaited us. They showered us with so much love. I was deeply moved by their display of affection. I felt grateful that after loving me as a film star all these years, they were placing the same faith in me as a political leader. I felt responsible towards them and did not want to let them down. The campaign journeys were very rigorous and draining. There were days it was very hot and stuffy and days when I craved for some respite. We were committed to a break-neck schedule and I was jumping in and out of helicopters. This was my first close interaction with my fans and it was both exciting as well as frightening. Gradually, I learnt to cope with it. I discovered that politics is a different world altogether and calls for a lot of hard work. We would begin our day at nine in the morning and return home past midnight. And this continued day after day till the end of the campaign,' she relates.

Every time Hema said 'yes' to something new, to something she felt unsure of in the beginning, the decision eventually proved an enriching experience. Whether it was sharing the platform with distinguished speakers to express her views on social issues or sharing the dais to give her views on lighter topics like being a vegetarian, Hema made sure to exploit all opportunities that came her way. She has dabbled in all the visual mediums – stage, cinema, television, and even commercials. She has endorsed products like tea, washing detergent, water purifier, mosquito repellent and also a cooperative bank. In her long career she has been bestowed with prominent titles on various platforms including the Padmashree. 'So many times we don't embrace experiences because we are scared of making mistakes. But it's only when we face challenges that we evolve and grow. It's all right not to be always successful. I guess what's in your destiny nobody can take away,' she says.

Her first project as an MP was to start a cleanliness and beautification drive at the Juhu Beach in Mumbai. Initiated by former colleague and MP, Shabana Azmi who endorsed a similar project in Bandra, Hema worked towards shifting the hawkers from the sand to the footpath. It was Hema's idea to beautify the place and build a park for the senior citizens and children. Hema has dreams to include another adjoining park for local artistes to perform in an open space and perhaps an amphitheatre to hold music concerts too. Another project Hema initiated was the pay-and-park facility for beach visitors. She wanted to do something for the National Park as well, particularly the often-reported leopard attacks on the residents of Borivali. As an animal lover (Hema has six dogs at home) she felt strongly about the issue. 'It is human beings who encroach on the animal space and later complain of danger to their lives. It is so unfair and insensitive. Mumbai is the only city to enjoy such a large forest area and we must do something to preserve our environment,' she says emphatically.

On a reflective note she agrees that politics is a jungle where destinies change every evening. 'When I joined the BJP a few years ago, it seemed like a party on the upswing. A few months down the line, the party had lost elections. Some people suggested that I quit BJP and join the rival camp. There was plenty of unsolicited advice. I listened to all but trusted none. I may not be a veteran in the field but I trust my instinct.' Hema adds that she does not know about the future but at the moment she is enjoying her role as a parliamentarian. Everytime she is in Delhi, her brother Jagannath accompanies her because Hema does not like being on her own, even though she stays in an apartment block where every resident is an MP. Hema says she looks forward to attending the sansad.

'There is so much to learn just by listening to what is being discussed even if at times the parliamentarians get unpleasant with each other. Within the four walls they are party members but outside, they interact as individuals, laugh and joke and party with each other. It's a different world altogether. Life in Delhi is very different from the film fraternity in Mumbai where everyone is so self-centred. It's only when you are exposed to the bigger world that you realize how constrained show business really is. Actors move around in the same camps and meet the same colleagues. They have little to offer each other in terms of enrichment. On the other hand, in my present surroundings there are new challenges every day ... As a member of the Parliament, it is my responsibility to bring up issues pertinent to the film fraternity. I have spoken about the government allotting some part of its budget for those in creative professions. I have put forward a petition for a retirement pension scheme for deserving artistes in the budget session. Several talented artistes in music and other fields live in penury. As a nation we honour them with awards like Padmashrees and Padmabhushans but what about their survival? Some of them are too old to fend for themselves

Hema's mother's presence at almost all her dance recitals instilled a sense of confidence in her.

'My mother was my friend, philosopher, critic and in a strange way my goal in life.' Hema sharing a special moment with her mother.

and some of them pursue art forms that are becoming extinct. The government must assume responsibility for these treasures of the country. Self-growth is all about getting the right exposure. I can sense I'm changing, becoming more aware. There are changes in my choice of the books I read and the kind of people I meet. I'm still wary of strangers befriending me but I'm more approachable now than I was in the past. To an extent it is the influence of the city. Delhi is an interesting place because something exciting is happening here all the time.'

On the personal front there is a feeling of remorse and longing for the departed ones. All the women who shielded and preserved her secrets in her younger days are no more. Shanta aunty, her escort for many years; Ma Indiraji who transformed her world view passed away on 31 December 1997; Saroja aunty, a loyal companion to Jaya Chakravarti for decades. And finally Hema's mother, the central person in her life.

For as long as she lived, the corner seat of the living room sofa was Jaya Chakravarti's privileged space. That was where she met Hema's producers in the earlier days. Even as her health deteriorated and her interactions with the film world became infrequent she still maintained the daily routine of coming down every morning, if only to supervise the domestic chores and oversee Hema's office staff. But gradually, she renounced all her responsibilities. Attended by a full-time nurse and followed by her two favourite dogs, Jaya Chakravarti preferred to spend her time watching television or snoozing. In fragile health for some time, Jaya was in her last days admitted to a nursing home where she succumbed to diabetes and cardiac arrest. She was seventy-four and the date was 24 June 2004. The entire family, including six grandchildren, was present during her last hours.

The home that once buzzed with relatives in large numbers is barren today. Hema who was the baby of the household is the new matriarch of the present family. She is happy that Dharmendra has found an outlet in politics. That Esha's career is looking up and Ahana has decided to become a filmmaker. 'It would have been nice if Amma was alive to see all this but her absence is something I must learn to deal with. A few days before she passed away, I had to report for a night shooting for my film *Veer Zaara*, which could not be cancelled. She did not want me to leave her side but I had to go and it made me feel miserable ...

'We had to admit her in the nursing home because she was to be put on the ventilator. Her leg was gravely infected with gangrene and we were trying to prevent infection from spreading further. She had slipped into a coma and these were difficult times for the entire family. I was shooting for *Kamini Damini* those days and would stop by on my way to the studio and back. She was sinking but something was holding her back … That's when my Reiki friends spoke to me … They said that unless I wholeheartedly relieved her, Amma would not die in peace … It was a traumatic decision for me. I delayed it as long as I could. Then on the night prior to her demise, I went late at night to the nursing home. They usually don't allow visitors in the ICU at that hour but I sought special permission. When I walked into the room it was past midnight. Her nurse was sitting beside her. I asked her to wait outside for sometime. Amma was breathing. She was semi-conscious. I knew she could not hear me, but had faith that she could sense my presence. I hugged her for long and whispered my gratitude in her ears … thanked her for all that she has given me … taught me … I sought her blessings … touched her feet and bid her goodbye … We have to part, I told her. It's the only way to end this suffering. A few hours later, I must have barely reached home, when we were asked to rush to the hospital. Amma was no more. She had taken her bow ... Today the only consolation is that her suffering is over … !'

In her mother's absence, for the first time, Hema reflected on the value of friendship. For many years she considered only her two sisters-in-law as her friends. 'And as time went by we came closer or let me put it this way that all of us have more time now because the current pace of life is less hectic. When I'm in town I enjoy spending time with my nephews and nieces ... In Delhi I spend all my free time with my other brother and sister-in-law. It is my firm belief that only those relationships which have no compulsions last forever. In a way Amma's passing away was the acid test for the family. The fact that the siblings have stuck together in her absence is a proof of our everlasting bond.'

Hema admits a bit disappointedly that she never sought friendship outside family. 'When girls of my age were making friends in school and college, I was busy with my dance and films. Still some people I came into contact with during those days proved loyal companions. My interior designer, Neetu Kohli was introduced to me by Manoj Kumar's wife Shashi, during the making of *Kranti*. She was designing Manoj Kumar's home and Shashi suggested that I try her out to design my home as well. My father assigned her to do my bedroom, which is by far the best room of the Juhu house. Large, airy and with an attached sitting room, overlooking the terrace where I have spent some beautiful moments of my life. The designing took a few months and during the process, we became friends. What drew me to Neetu was that my father, who seldom approved of strangers, became very fond of her. When I became pregnant, she was the only outsider Dharamji and I let into the secret. Over the years Neetu and I have shared several confidences on many a quiet evening …

'The beauty of life never ceases to surprise me. I'm discovering new friends from different fields of life and have over the years formed a strong support group. My two sisters-in-law, Prabha and Smita are first my friends and later relatives. Prabha is the eldest amongst us but is the most mischievous. She is drawn to reading and writing and heads the *seetaandgeeta.com* website that offers guidance to women in distress. She has also written a series of self-help booklets. Smita is sedate, observant and always helpful. She is very skilful in household activities and dependable in a crisis. There is a healing quality to her. They are temperamentally different and I cherish my relationship with both.'

Hema is also appreciative of the efforts and support of her two cousins, Prabha and Mohan (Shanta aunty's children) who have been a part of the family since their formative years. Both have grown up before her and are as precious to her as her own siblings. While Mohan got married and built his own nest, he continues to look after Hema's productions (films and television). He supervises her day-to-day office work and escorts Hema wherever she travels for her election campaigns. His elder sister Prabha, addressed as Pappu by the family, is a devoted companion to Hema, both at home and outside. She is a part of Hema's Natyavihar Kala Kendra dance troupe and plays a major role in the execution of their dance rehearsals. As a dancer, Prabha has

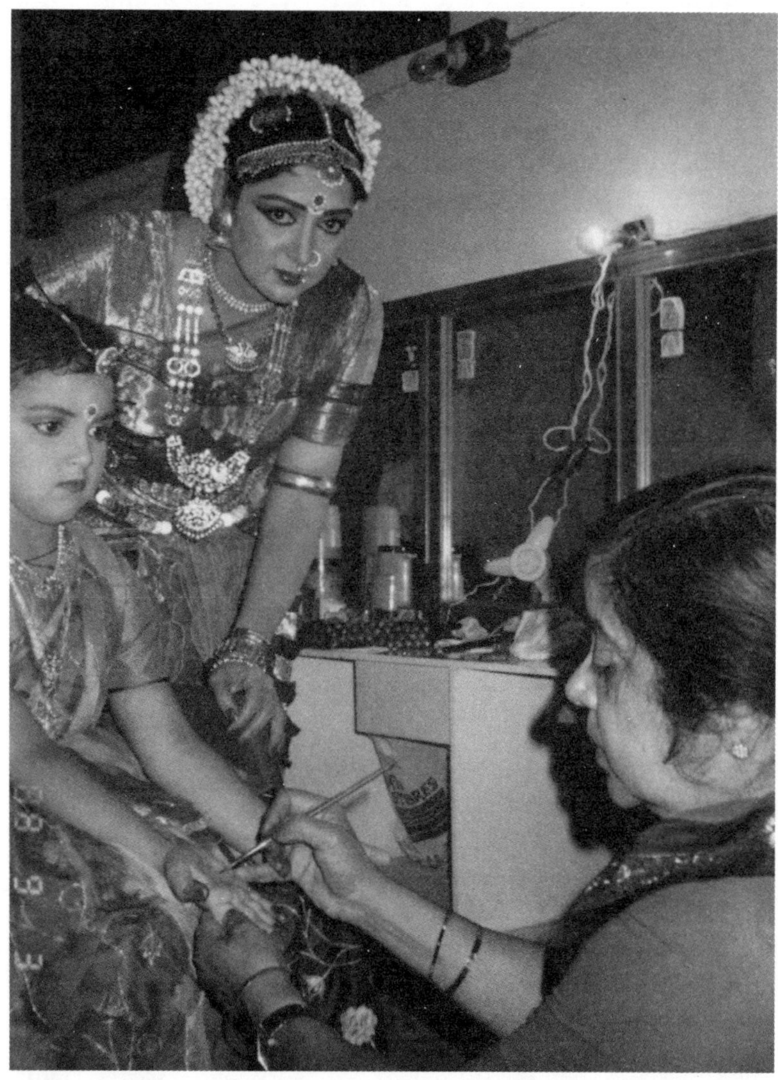

Family Tradition: *Applying aalta on Hema's feet and palms before a performance was always Jaya's prerogative. Jaya here is applying aalta on her little granddaughter Esha's palms.*

always come forward to play negative characters and performs them with conviction. She was Kaikeyi and Surpanakha in *Ramayan;* Uda, Meera's sister-in-law in *Meera;* Rati in *Durga;* Putana in *Yashoda Krishna* and Mahakali in *Mahalakshmi.*

In *Draupadi* Prabha plays Maya, a companion sent by Lord Krishna to comfort Draupadi in turbulent times. In real life too Prabha plays an extension of Maya – always by her cousin's side when she needs her. When Hema launched herself as a director in her teleserial *Noopur* and later her debut film *Dil Aashna Hai,* Prabha helped as her first assistant. Hema's relationship with both her cousins has weathered many phases but emerged stronger each time, surviving three decades.

Hema makes special mention of Mehta *saab*, her manager for three decades. She came into contact with him in 1971 while shooting for *Bhai Ho To Aisa* where Mehta served as the production in-charge. The Chakravartis kept in touch with him and sought his advice in matters related to Hema's career. In the early 1980s as Hema rose to super stardom, Hema and her mother felt the need for a full-time secretary and since a foundation of trust was already formed with Mehta, he was the obvious choice. Since then Mehta has been with Hema and now co-ordinates all activities of Natyavihar Kala Kendra. 'Over the years, we have had several creative arguments but when I look back, I cannot imagine my journey without his unflinching support,' says Hema.

Besides the family and Neetu Kohli, Hema's list of other friends include Maureen, who introduced her to the Art of Living, Nisha, who designs a section of her clothes, Anupam who exposed her to the world of aviation and to various related experiences she did not explore at the right stage of her life, and Surdasji for guiding her on the path of spirituality. 'It's a different equation with different friends – serious communication with some and joyous moments like going out for dinners and drives or meeting up at each other's home, with others. Simple joys but very precious.' Hema also has many political friends with whom she shares her views on various issues.

At the crossroads of life, Hema is overcome by nostalgia when she looks back on her debut performance as a six-year-old when her mother applied the *aalta* (red colour) on her palms and feet, 'Over the years no matter where I performed, this special gesture remained Amma's privilege. On the day I was performing with Kelucharan Mahapatra, I insisted she apply the *aalta* for me as a good omen. Her hands were trembling but she managed to paint a not-so-round circle on my feet. It was a precious moment for me. That show is memorable since both Amma and guruji are no more today. During the performance I saw the transformation of a seventy-year-old artiste into a seventeen-year-old Krishna. It was sheer magic and to think that there will never be another Kelucharan Mahapatra ... It saddens me that I will never get a chance to dance with him again ... Though not my dance guru, I will miss the thespian as a magnificent artiste and I'm certain that nobody can replace him in my life. It breaks my heart that Amma will never apply the *aalta* on my palms ... It has been a few years since her death but I think of her at the oddest moments. It's difficult to let go off memories ... Attachment is a painful emotion.'

Sometimes, Hema wonders if life would have been different had she married an IAS officer or a top rank engineer, the kind of person her father would have wanted for her. Then, may be she would have settled down in Chennai or the US, spent her time dishwashing in a swanky apartment or perhaps running a dance school. 'I'm not sure if I would have liked to live that kind of life. I'm not sure if I would have been happy being away from show business ... Cinema and the city of Mumbai have been a part of my growing up and being away from them would have left a vacuum.'

Many years ago, Waheeda Rehman had stated that marriage is a complicated chapter in the life of a film actress. It does not affect the life of an actor but if the actress takes too long to settle down, it is tough to find the right life partner. Hema confirms this and recommends that heroines keen on settling down must do so before they turn thirty. Later, it becomes difficult to start a family.

'Career is important, and one can pursue it after marriage and children, provided the partner and circumstances are favourable but it is not worth sacrificing one's personal life. At the end of the day, you need someone beside you to share your life and thoughts,' she asserts.

Hema admits a trifle hesitantly that she was denied many such moments. 'The best of partners drift away with time because of the lack of passion, and in my case he was already committed when we came together. Of course, there are deprivations. There are many occasions you want him to be with you, to share your special moments and he is not there. There are special moments in your children's life, and again, he has prior commitments. There are milestones in your career and his, and one is not together because making an appearance together becomes a statement. It makes other loved ones uneasy, so you have to withdraw, understand, let go and swallow your hurt ... and you do just that! When I was younger, it would hurt terribly. I would feel, is this the togetherness for which I went through so much … waited so long … ?'

Over the years, the pain has lessened gradually or perhaps Hema has matured and accepted her circumstances gracefully. 'The misgivings will always remain as my father had rightly predicted but the aching loss has been substituted by a new identity and reassurance. Today, I value my space and self-worth and nobody can destroy that … '

Spirituality is a state of mind and as a little girl, Hema remembers attending *satsangs* held in her neighbourhood accompanied by her parents. Later, when her brothers and she were growing up, her parents frequently visited Tirupati temple where they participated in the *abhisheks*. Practising meditation and yoga comes naturally to her and therefore she admires the philosophy of Sri Sri Ravi Shankar, 'The reason so many people flock to see him is because he heals the anguished.' Hema admits that while Ma remains omnipresent in her life, she has reverence for Sri Sri Ravi Shankar. She also has high regard for the *sadhana* of Baba Ramdev and accepts that there has to be something about the philosophy of religious leaders like Morari Bapu or Satya Sai Baba for so many people to be drawn to them. 'It cannot be just charisma or the art of oratory. There has to be a bigger meaning to their presence because they resolve something for us that ordinary people cannot,' she muses.

Hema maintains that only a truly content and confident disciple has no complexes in appreciating other gurus because they don't come in the way of her bonding with her guruma. She says that even though Ma is no more, she feels her presence all the time and her sense of well-being originates from her. 'It is said that you find a guru when you are ready for one. I'm fortunate that I found Ma Indiraji when I needed her the most. Often you are not conscious until an episode transforms your life. It's only when you come face to face with adversities that you discover fortitude. Many a time you are unable to cope with travesties, you lose courage. At moments like these it helps to have a guru. If he is the right guru, he helps you sail through your calamities …

'A spiritual guru can change the course of a person's life. All of us need someone to put things in the right perspective for us and only a guru can do that. Even someone as enlightened as my guruma needed a guide. She was fortunate to discover Dilip Kumar Roy, a disciple of Sri Aurobindo. Wherever I travel, I carry my devotional books and deities with me and no matter how long it takes, I don't leave my home for shooting or other meetings without my morning puja …

'Once you accept the reality, things are never that painful. I accept my destiny … I cannot get everything. At that moment, when Dharamji and I agreed to come together, marriage was the only solution. We shared a few good years together and the result is our two beautiful daughters. Today, I'm not alone. I have all their support. Besides, I've evolved as a person and have learnt to look at events in life more spiritually. I console myself that had I been into a regular marriage with the regular responsibilities of other wives, would I have been able to evolve and grow the way did? Would I have been able to nurture my dance and other artistic journeys the way I have? Would I have explored the numerous opportunities and enhanced myself? Would I have been able to nurse my ailing mother and aunts? Connect with, and support my cousins? Would I have travelled such a long path, dabbled with so many mediums the way I do today? I feel I was able to do all this because I had my own space. Dharamji trusted me and encouraged my pursuits. Always concerned and demonstrative in our private space, his reassurance has instilled confidence in me. With time he has evolved too. These days he is regularly practicing yoga and has taken a fascination to writing poetry. He is back to acting in films once again and learning the ropes in politics. We cherish the time we spend together and discuss our new projects and children. He recites his poems to me and I tell him about my new ballets and also about the new flower that has blossomed in my garden.'

Hema says that dance helps her as an exercise. 'I have always been restless by nature and the slightest disorder can make me fly off the handle. But I am changing ... Earlier, when I was upset I would just get into my car and drive off. These days I have imbibed the art of healing others and myself with Reiki and it has transformed my life. Everyday is a new experience and it's only when one is detached that one can view turbulence from a distance. There is a karmic reason for everything that occurs, so why analyse everything? We don't want to accept it but there is a lot to learn and grow from observing nature. The Art of Living emphasizes on meditation and if you do it sincerely it does heal you. Ma Indiraji is gone, but I'm trying to tread the path she showed me. My pursuit is to live a life without expectations and regret. Not easy, but it is the only way to purify the soul,' she elaborates.

Perhaps Jaya Chakravarti was prophetic in naming her daughter Hema Malini. Perhaps it was predestined that she should not adorn a surname (Chakravarti in the maiden days and Deol after marriage). Perhaps it is in Hema Malini's destiny to walk alone ...

Notes from a Mother's Diary

Jaya Chakravarti was a regular contributor in Tamil magazines and has to her credit several books including the Tamil translation of Tulsidas's *Ramayan*. It is said that she woke up before dawn, and not to get distracted from her routine, wrote feverishly till daybreak. A woman of varied interests she was a writer, singer, painter, but primarily a proud wife and mother. The film fraternity perceived her as a formidable force.

Every time her high-heeled sandals clicked on the wooden staircase of their Juhu bungalow, film producers waiting in the living room sat up alert. There was something commanding about her personality. Hema's directors and heroes remember her as a forceful woman who always had her way. The family describes her as a compassionate matriarch who went out of her way to help the talented and deserving. According to them she put up a stern facade only to safeguard herself and her daughter from the wild world of films. Her son-in-law Dharmendra, credits her for everything that Hema and her granddaughters stand for today.

Facing Page: *'A mother shares a beautiful relationship with her child.' In a still from her ballet* Yashoda Krishna.

Here are some excerpts from Jaya Chakravarti's journal, which she showed me just a few months before she passed away, where she recounts Hema's fascinating five-decade-long journey.

... When you are pregnant, you feel closer to God. I have an intuition; I just know I'm going to have a daughter. When I hold the little one in my arms for the first time I feel instinctively that she is going to be an artiste.

... Hema is five and I enrol her in a dance school. She is the youngest in her class. Her limbs are delicate and she can barely follow the steps. But it does not matter. She will learn by and by.

... She has picked up a few steps but does not seem very interested in dance. I have to keep her motivated everyday. She does not protest openly but I can sense she resists it. But because she is an obedient child, she follows the instructions of her elders. Everyday, after school, she knows she has to dedicate an hour or two to dance.

... It's not true that my husband Chakravarti is against Hema pursuing dance. In fact, he encourages her whole-heartedly. As a

V.S.R. Chakravarti and Jaya Chakravarti with Hema: *Her parents devoted themselves and their life for the dreams they had cherished for their daughter.*

government officer residing in the capital, he is well connected. A lot of invitations for these concerts come from his circle of friends.

... Hema is nine and she is one of the few child dancers recognized in the capital. She is frequently invited for stage performances. Though a trifle nervous prior to a show, she does not make it apparent. That has been a habit with her. I'm nervous too but never show it. She understands that I want her to do well and she obliges.

... It's a big day for all of us. It is Hema's first dance performance at the Rashtrapati Bhavan in Delhi and she is really very good.

... Pursuing any art is an expensive exercise but I manage somehow. Part of the money comes from my husband, some I set aside from household expenditure and some by selling my jewellery. I have a beautiful gold belt presented to me on my wedding day by my father. It is my *Streedhan*. I mortgage the belt each time I need the money and redeem it when I'm better off.

... Grooming Hema takes up a lot of my time but it is never at the expense of my other children's time. I'm more attentive to Hema because she is very young and needs to be escorted.

... It is my dream to make Hema a very famous dancer and she will succeed because she is gifted. One look at her and you know that she is an artiste.

... Hema is being offered films and we are considering the proposals. Some people warn us that the film industry is not a safe place for a decent family like us. But something tells me it is the right decision. I'm not sure what destiny holds in store for Hema. I'm not sure if she can fit into her new surrounding. We come from a different background, but producer Anantha Swamy has promised to be our guide. Promised to be by our side all the time.

... Hema has had a few releases and her career is looking up. She has to do all kinds of dances on screen but she has the rare ability to perform the most bizarre movements with immense grace. Also it's not as if all her screen dances are ordinary. Time and again she gets exquisite numbers, some of them based on pure classical form.

... The big screen demands that she puts on plenty of make-up. It is to protect her skin from the lights and camera. But as a result she looks too pink on screen. I disapprove of her over made-up face. Until she joined films, I would personally supervise her make-up and dress her for every performance. Now she has a personal hairdresser, make-up man and a costume designer as well. She uses the same staff for her dance shows. But applying the *aalta* on her palms and feet is my privilege. This has remained a tradition with us for years.

... Hema is on a long outdoor shoot and I have sent her guruji to the location for rehearsals. There are times I personally fly with him to the city where she is shooting. Dancers cannot afford to be out of touch with their art. A few days without rehearsals can make her body go rigid.

... My sons are doing well in their respective jobs and Hema's career is soaring. Dance is not an invasion in her film career. Her directors have no complaints. She has never cancelled shootings for a show and if her guruji is visiting on location, he takes lessons only after her pack-up. She is often tired and wants to sleep but I insist that an extra hour and a half of exercise will not make a difference. After rehearsal, she has dinner and drops off to sleep.

... Her diary is crowded with too many films and shows. I sometimes fear that a time will come when she will not be able to manage both but she is in good health and is motivated to juggle the two. She also knows that I'm stubborn and I will not give up on her easily. Even my husband had to give in to me.

... Hema's detractors say that she receives dance invitations only because she is a film star. I disagree, I feel that she is talented and is extraordinarily lucky. While she was still in her teens, she performed before Pandit Nehru and Dr Radhakrishnan. In fact, she is the only dancer who has performed in the presence of every president of the country, right up to R. Venkatraman.

Esha and Ahana: Daughters who have brought in happiness and contentment.

... Hema is a fine danseuse and credit is due to her. She is slender and moves gracefully and has an expressive face to match. She is improving everyday, both on screen as well as on stage. It's true that many people come to watch her shows only because she is a famous star but that is the price of stardom she has to pay.

... Everybody says Hema Malini is very beautiful. What they don't realize is that her beauty is more internal than external. She is spiritual and this serenity reflects on her face. She is non-materialistic. I know this since I have handled her accounts as long as I was in good health. Now, she does it herself.

... Marriage and motherhood suits Hema. I've never seen her as content as with her two babies. Dharmendra is a good son-in-law, respectful towards me and considerate towards the family. Whenever I feel the girls are getting out of hand or Hema is over-indulging them, I ask him to intervene. He relies on my wisdom, compliments me as the best influence on my daughter and grandchildren.

... Over the years dance has evolved and so has Hema. In the earlier days, she performed solo Bharatanatyam dance recitals. Later, she introduced ballets because she didn't want to restrict her audience. It was a good decision because today she does not have the strength she had twenty years ago. She needs to take a break in between her acts and this is the time the other dancers fill the gaps.

... Hema is very keen that Esha and Ahana learn dance but I feel they are not inclined. Hema is disheartened and tries every trick in the book to get them interested. When I tell her to leave them alone, she gets angry with me. 'Did you give up on me when I was not inclined?' she asks. I didn't but times were different then.

... I'm in the auditorium for yet another performance of Hema. As the curtain is about to rise, I recall the little girl at Rashtrapati Bhavan. Hema has come a long way since then. In the olden days my husband used to announce her dance items on stage. Today, my older son Kannan anchors her shows. I am proud that both of us did not give up despite all obstacles. I expected her to succeed, but to be honest I did not expect the magic to sustain for so many years.

... I was in the audience on the occasion of Esha and Ahana's debut shows and today they perform with their mother. I'm hoping that Hema has groomed them adequately. I cannot comment on my grandchildren's performance for I don't follow Odissi as well as Bharatanatyam.

... There are some reports in the newspapers comparing my granddaughters to Hema. It's not fair. They are still young and have a long way to go. Hema has been dancing for the last thirty years. Times are different too. In the olden days, there were not as many distractions as exist today. When Hema was young, she had to divide her time just between her school and dance. When she became older, it was between films and dance. Esha and Ahana have dance, career ambitions and so many more interests. This generation is all the time busy with friends. Hema had no friends.

... Esha is shooting round the clock and on her free days hardly seen at home. These days Ahana is busy too. She has enrolled for a film direction course in New York and Hema has granted permission. I disagree with the decision, feel she is too young to be left alone in a foreign country but nobody listens. I confide my fears to my son-in-law. He assumes responsibility for Ahana's safety. I'm reassured. Whenever he promises something, he always keeps his word.

... Hema tells me that she sometimes feels that she hasn't been as good a mother to her girls as I was to her. That is not true. They share a different relationship. She gives them a lot more freedom than I ever gave her. My husband and I were very strict.

A Family Photograph: *Hema with her parents and brothers at her elder brother Kannan's wedding with Prabha.*

My children were scared of us. Her children love her dearly but I don't think they are scared of her. I worked very hard to sustain her career. She works doubly hard, to sustain her own career and her daughters' future.

Epilogue

It is late in the evening and Hema Malini is in her bedroom, jet lagged from her recent trip to the US. Downstairs, her office buzzes with activity. A while later, Hema descends the wooden staircase. The housemaid hands her a packet of jasmine flowers wrapped in green leaves. She opens the bundle, inhales the fragrance, and winds it around her hair. 'Amma loved flowers and wore them everyday. I've continued the tradition after her demise. Irrespective of whether I'm in town or not, fresh flowers come home every evening,' she says steeped in nostalgia.

She settles in her favourite seat in the living room facing the door. Her mother's picture is displayed prominently on the table. Hema points to the vacant seat beside her and says, 'That was Amma's seat and everyone respected that. We light a lamp before Amma's photograph every evening. It makes us feel that she is still with us ... It is strange but for days after she was gone, I longed for a moment to connect with her even if it was just a fleeting glance. But it never happened. I often talked to her in my silent moments but could never recapture her in my mind. Then one day, close to her first death anniversary, I was alone in the US and suddenly she appeared in my dream. Looking younger, smiling she passed by the verandah, dressed in a peach pink sari. Her long, lustrous hair was damp after a shower and left loose, like in the old days. She seemed at peace with herself. I turned to stop her but she just walked past even though her fragrance lingered … I woke up from my sleep startled. I immediately called up my brothers and told them about my dream. Clearly the vision had a message for her children. It was Amma's way of telling us that she is alright and we should also carry on with our lives …

'It is always the eldest in the family who keeps the rest united. My brothers and I came closer in Amma's last days. My sisters-in-law have always been protective about me but after she has gone they are all the more concerned. Somehow it has become a tradition that whenever any of us in the family is disturbed, we sit beside Amma's photograph and feel healed. Whether we accept it or not, there is an external force guiding us. One does not want to believe these things but there is a positive energy with a healing touch. It's up to us to recognize these signs,' she states.

For a long time Hema had been thinking of shifting to the new bungalow her husband had built for her over a decade ago. Dharmendra was on his way to shooting in Filmcity when he had spotted this plot surrounded by beautiful lush green trees. The next day he contacted the builder and confirmed the deal. Gradually he began the construction of the bungalow and later the landscape of the garden. The dream home designed by friend Neetu Kohli has been ready for some time but it took a while for Hema and her two daughters, firmly entrenched in their old home, to shift to the new address. Finally, Hema made up her mind and the daughters had to follow. It has been only a few months that they have moved in but they thoroughly enjoy their new surroundings.

In her Juhu home Hema seldom spent any time in her garden. At her new residence, 39 Yashodham Enclave in Goregaon, the patio outside the living room adjoining the garden is her favourite spot. There, Jaya Chakravarti's picture occupied a corner of the living room table. In her present home Hema has placed her mother and her guruma's pictures inside her temple beside her three favourite goddesses – Lakshmi, Saraswati and Durga.

The four-storeyed bungalow overlooks a sprawling garden. Drooping branches are sprinkled with fragrant colourful flowers. 'Dharamji was adamant that not a single tree should be felled during the construction and that is the beauty of this place. It is a treat to wake up in the morning and be surrounded with greenery all around. Every room has a picturesque view … There are so many lessons to be learnt from nature. We need to nurture relationships. Children need to be nurtured like growing plants. The slightest negligence in the manure or watering and the mistakes stare back at you. I've always loved children and wanted to get married because I wanted to have children. I've been through many highs and lows but everything has been worth it because of my two daughters …

'The relationship between a mother and daughter is the most unique relationship. The camaraderie, the little caring gestures, and the intimacy and bonding as they grow up is special. My relationship with my mother, though intimate, was not of equals. Amma was in total control of my life. She protected me, nurtured me until I was able to take care of myself. Today's children, however, need their space and it's good because they need to mature and learn some home truths on their own. I have granted my daughters their space by not monitoring their every move and at the same time being accessible to them,' she philosophizes. She compares relationships to sand held in an open palm. It stands in a heap but slips out of the fingers when you try to hold it in your fist. 'All healthy relationships demand space and the skill is in acquiring that without losing intimacy. And Dharamji has this rare ability ...

'The joy of watching your children grow and prosper is fulfilling for a mother. They are my world and they know it … I have no complaints with life because all my dreams have been realized.'

Recently one night, as Hema lay awake she wondered how Krishna guides us through life ... 'Our mythology has constant reference to his childhood, then adolsence, and later old age ... He is the perfect God, the perfect child to Yashoda, the perfect lover to Radha, the perfect friend to Draupadi, and finally the perfect obsession for the devoted Meera.' The thought made Hema concieve *Krishna Ras,* a unique two-day dance festival devoted to the versatality and dynamism of the alluring Lord.

Hema's zest for life and attraction for adventure is admirable. At 50-plus she is still wooed to endorse products, still chased by big banners for acting assignments. Hema admits that she loves the smell of grease paint and basks in the arc lights but equally looks forward to her political campaigns in remote regions and the lively parliamentary sessions in Delhi. 'The old home where I grew up in Gole Market as a child is just a few miles away from my present MP residence in Delhi ... but it took me years to reach here ...' Today an average day in her life is packed with myriad appointments ranging from dance rehearsals to commitments on social issues. She is also the brand ambassador for 'Ekal Vidyalaya' run by Friends of Tribal Society, and 'Vision 20/20' an organization that works for the visually impaired. Clearly her cup is full to the brim but Hema's spirit to forever chase challenges is almost seductive, her effort to seek simple joys in the severest crisis almost child-like. Her commitment to politics, films, and dance keep her occupied. As she herself feels, 'This is the busiest phase of my life but I'm enjoying every moment of it.'

Thirty-seven years ago when Hema's godfather Anantha Swamy transported an almond-eyed awkward adolescent from Chennai to Mumbai, nobody had envisioned that she would, one day, conquer the fantasies of the masses. Her godfather, however, was determined to turn the native beauty into a superstar. Weeks prior to her debut release he launched a mammoth publicity campaign where every poster in the city was plastered with working stills of Hema Malini from *Sapno Ka Saudagar* with a caption below reading 'Dream Girl comes to town'.

A star was born in 1969 and three and a half decades later, continues her reign over the hearts of millions of her fans.

At fifty-seven, Hema Malini is the only star to be still referred to as the Dream Girl …

Fact File

I. FILMS

(1968) *Sapno Ka Saudagar*
Producer: Screen Gems; Director: Mahesh Kaul;
Co-star: Raj Kapoor

(1969) *Jahan Pyar Mile*
Producer: LR Films
Director: Lekh Tandon
Co-star: Shashi Kapoor

(1969) *Waaris*
Producer: Vasu Films
Director: Ramanna
Co-stars: Jeetendra, Mehmood

(1970) *Abhinetri*
Producer: Subodh Mukherji Productions
Director: Subodh Mukherji
Co-star: Shashi Kapoor

(1970) *Aansoo Aur Muskaan*
Producer: B. Anantha Swamy
Director: P. Madhavan
Co-star: Ajay Sahni

(1970) *Johnny Mera Naam*
Producer: Gulshan Rai

Director: Vijay Anand
Co-star: Dev Anand

(1970) *Sharafat*
Producer: Madan Mohla
Director: Asit Sen
Co-star: Dharmendra

(1970) *Tum Haseen Main Jawan*
Producer: Bhappi Sonie
Director: Bhappi Sonie
Co-star: Dharmendra

(1971) *Andaaz*
Producer: G.P. Sippy
Director: Ramesh Sippy
Co-stars: Shammi Kapoor, Simi Garewal, Rajesh Khanna

(1971) *Lal Pathar*
Producer: F.C. Mehra
Director: Sushil Majumdar
Co-stars: Vinod Mehra, Raakhee, Raaj Kumar

(1971) *Naya Zamana*
Producer: Pramod Chakraborty
Director: Pramod Chakraborty
Co-stars: Dharmendra, Aruna Irani

(1971) *Paraya Dhan*
Producer: Rajendra Bhatia
Director: Rajendra Bhatia
Co-stars: Rakesh Roshan, Balraj Sahni

(1971) *Tere Mere Sapne*
Producer: Vijay Anand
Director: Vijay Anand
Co-stars: Dev Anand, Mumtaz

(1972) *Babul Ki Galiyaan*
Producer: S.D. Narang
Director: S.D. Narang
Co-stars: Sanjay Khan, Shatrughan Sinha

(1972) *Bhai Ho To Aisa*
Producer: A.K. Nadiadwala
Director: Manmohan Desai
Co-stars: Jeetendra, Shatrughan Sinha

(1972) *Gora Aur Kala*
Producer: Raj Kumar Kohli
Director: Naresh Kumar
Co-stars: Rajendra Kumar, Rekha

(1972) *Raja Jaani*
Producer: Madan Mohla
Director: Mohan Sehgal
Co-star: Dharmendra

(1972) *Seeta Aur Geeta*
Producer: G.P. Sippy
Director: Ramesh Sippy
Co-stars: Dharmendra, Sanjeev Kumar

(1973) *Chhupa Rustam*
Producer: Vijay Anand
Director: Vijay Anand
Co-stars: Dev Anand, Vijay Anand

(1973) *Gehri Chaal*
Producer: Chitralaya
Director: Sridhar
Co-stars: Jeetendra, Amitabh Bachchan

(1973) *Joshila*
Producer: Gulshan Rai
Director: Yash Chopra
Co-stars: Dev Anand, Raakhee

(1973) *Jugnu*
Producer: Pramod Chakraborty
Director: Pramod Chakraborty
Co-star: Dharmendra

(1973) *Shareef Badmash*
Producer: Dev Anand
Director: Raj Khosla
Co-star: Dev Anand

(1974) *Amir Garib*
Producer: Mohan Kumar
Director: Mohan Kumar
Co-star: Dev Anand

(1974) *Dost*
Producer: Premji

Director: Dulal Guha
Co-stars: Dharmendra, Shatrughan Sinha

(1974) *Dulhan*
Producer: B. Anandawali
Director: C.V. Rajendran
Co-star: Jeetendra

(1974) *Haath Ki Safai*
Producer: I.A. Nadiadwala
Director: Prakash Mehra
Co-stars: Simi Garewal, Vinod Khanna, Randhir Kapoor

(1974) *Kasauti*
Producer: Arbind Sen
Director: Arbind Sen
Co-star: Amitabh Bachchan

(1974) *Patthar Aur Payal*
Producer: N.P. Singh
Director: Harmesh Malhotra
Co-stars: Dharmendra, Vinod Khanna

(1974) *Prem Nagar*
Producer: D. Rama Naidu
Director: K.S. Prakash Rao
Co-star: Rajesh Khanna

(1975) *Dharmatma*
Producer: Feroz Khan
Director: Feroz Khan
Co-stars: Feroz Khan, Rekha

(1975) *Do Thug*
Producer: S.D. Narang
Director: S.D. Narang
Co-star: Shatrughan Sinha

(1975) *Khushboo*
Producer: Prasan Kapoor
Director: Gulzar
Co-stars: Jeetendra, Sharmila Tagore

(1975) *Pratigya*
Producer: Vikramjeet Productions
Director: Dulal Guha
Co-star: Dharmendra

(1975) *Sanyasi*
Producer: Sohanlal Kanwar
Director: Sohanlal Kanwar
Co-star: Manoj Kumar
(1975) *Sholay*
Producer: G.P. Sippy; Director: Ramesh Sippy
Co-stars: Dharmendra, Amitabh Bachchan,
Sanjeev Kumar, Jaya Bachchan, Amjad Khan
(1975) *Sunehra Sansar*
Producer: Vadde Sobhanadri, ASR Anjanyelu
Director: A. Subba Rao
Co-stars: Rajendra Kumar, Mala Sinha
(1976) *Aap Beeti*
Producer: Mohan Kumar
Director: Mohan Kumar
Co-stars: Shashi Kapoor, Ashok Kumar, Nirupa Roy
(1976) *Charas*
Producer: Ramanand Sagar
Director: Ramanand Sagar
Co-star: Dharmendra
(1976) *Dus Numbri*
Producer: Madan Mohla
Director: Madan Mohla
Co-star: Manoj Kumar
(1976) *Jaaneman*
Producer: Dev Anand
Director: Chetan Anand
Co-star: Dev Anand
(1976) *Maa*
Producer: M.M.A. Chinnappa Devar
Director: M.A. Thirumugam
Co-star: Dharmendra
(1976) *Mehbooba*
Producer: Mushir Riaz
Director: Shakti Samanta
Co-star: Rajesh Khanna
(1976) *Naach Utha Sansar*
Producer: Mohmud Sarosh

Director: Yakub Hussain
Co-stars: Simi Garewal, Shashi Kapoor

(1976) *Sharafat Chhod Di Maine*
Producer: Damodar Menon
Director: Jagdev Bhambri
Co-stars: Feroz Khan, Neetu Singh

(1977) *Chacha Bhatija*
Producer: Baldev Pushkarna
Director: Manmohan Desai
Co-stars: Dharmendra, Randhir Kapoor, Yogeeta Bali,

(1977) *Dhoop Chhaon*
Producer: S.N. Jain
Director: Prahlad Sharma
Co-stars: Sanjeev Kumar, Yogeeta Bali

(1977) *Dream Girl*
Producer: R.K. Chakraborty and J.K. Behl
Director: Pramod Chakraborty
Co-star: Dharmendra

(1977) *Kinara*
Producer: Pranlal Mehta, Gulzar
Director: Gulzar
Co-star: Jeetendra, Dharmendra

(1977) *Palkon Ki Chhaon Mein*
Producer: Nariman I. Baria, A. Khalia
Director: Meraj
Co-star: Rajesh Khanna

(1977) *Tinku*
Producer: Parvez
Director: Navin Pics
Co-stars: Tinku, Rajesh Khanna

(1978) *Azaad*
Producer: Pramod Chakraborty
Director: Pramod Chakraborty
Co-star: Dharmendra

(1978) *Apna Khoon*
Producer: S.K. Kapur
Director: B. Subhash
Co-star: Shashi Kapoor

(1978) *Dillagi*
Producer: Bikram Singh Deol
Director: Basu Chatterji
Co-star: Dharmendra, Mithu Mukherjee

(1978) *Trishul*
Producer: Gulshan Rai; Director: Yash Chopra
Co-stars: Amitabh Bachchan,
Sanjeev Kumar, Shashi Kapoor, Raakhee

(1979) *Dil Ka Heera*
Producer: Manian, Vidwan, V. Laxman
Director: Dulal Guha
Co-star: Dharmendra

(1979) *Hum Tere Aashiq Hain*
Producer: Prem Sagar
Director: Prem Sagar
Co-star: Jeetendra

(1979) *Meera*
Producer: Premji
Director: Gulzar
Co-stars: Vinod Khanna, Shammi Kapoor, Vidya Sinha

(1979) *Ratnadeep*
Producer: R. Kannan, Jagannath
Director: Basu Chatterji
Co-star: Girish Karnad

(1980) *Aas Paas*
Producer: Jagdish Kumar
Director: J. Om Prakash
Co-star: Dharmendra

(1980) *Alibaba Aur 40 Chor*
Producer: F.C. Mehra
Director: Umesh Mehra
Co-stars: Dharmendra, Zeenat Aman

(1980) *Bandish*
Producer: D. Rama Naidu
Director: K. Bapaiah
Co-star: Rajesh Khanna

(1980) *Do Aur Do Paanch*
Producer: C. Dhandayuthpani

Director: Rakesh Kumar
Co-stars: Amitabh Bachchan, Shashi Kapoor, Parveen Babi

(1980) *The Burning Train*
Producer: B.R. Films; Director: Ravi Chopra
Co-stars: Dharmendra, Jeetendra, Vinod Khanna, Vinod Mehra, Neetu Singh, Parveen Babi

(1981) *Dard*
Producer: Shyam Sunder Shivdasani
Director: Ambrish Sangal
Co-stars: Rajesh Khanna, Poonam Dhillon

(1981) *Jyoti*
Producer: Pramod Chakraborty
Director: Pramod Chakraborty
Co-stars: Jeetendra, Ashok Kumar

(1981) *Kranti*
Producer: Manoj Kumar; Director: Manoj Kumar
Co-stars: Manoj Kumar, Dilip Kumar, Parveen Babi, Shashi Kapoor, Shatrughan Sinha

(1981) *Krodhi*
Producer: Ranjit Virk
Director: Subhash Ghai
Co-stars: Dharmendra, Zeenat Aman, Shashi Kapoor

(1981) *Kudrat*
Producer: B.S. Khanna; Director: Chetan Anand
Co-stars: Vinod Khanna, Rajesh Khanna, Raaj Kumar, Priya Rajvansh

(1981) *Maan Gaye Ustad*
Producer: S.K. Kapur
Director: Shibu Mitra
Co-star: Shashi Kapoor

(1981) *Meri Aawaz Suno*
Producer: G.A. Seshagiri Rao
Director: S.V. Rajendra Singh
Co-star: Jeetendra

(1981) *Naseeb*
Producer: Manmohan Desai; Director: Manmohan Desai
Co-stars: Amitabh Bachchan, Shatrughan Sinha, Rishi Kapoor, Reena Roy, Kim

(1981) *Satte Pe Satta*
Producer: Romu N. Sippy
Director: Raj Sippy
Co-star: Amitabh Bachchan

(1982) *Baghawat*
Producer: Ramanand Sagar
Director: Ramanand Sagar
Co-stars: Dharmendra, Reena Roy

(1982) *Desh Premi*
Producer: Subhash Desai
Director: Manmohan Desai
Co-stars: Amitabh Bachchan, Uttam Kumar

(1982) *Justice Choudhary*
Producer: G.A. Seshagiri
Director: K. Raghavendra Rao
Co-stars: Jeetendra, Sridevi, Moushumi Chatterjee

(1982) *Farz Aur Kanoon*
Producer: Roja Pictures
Director: K. Raghavendra Rao
Co-stars: Jeetendra, Rati Agnihotri

(1982) *Meherbani*
Producer: Ajit Singh Deol
Director: A. Narang
Co-stars: Dharmendra, Sarika

(1982) *Rajput*
Producer: Mushir Riaz
Director: Vijay Anand
Co-stars: Dharmendra, Rajesh Khanna, Vinod Khanna

(1982) *Samrat*
Producer: Madan Mohla
Director: Mohan Sehgal
Co-stars: Dharmendra, Jeetendra

(1982) *Do Dishayen*
Producer: R. Renuka
Director: Dulal Guha
Co-star: Dharmendra

(1983) *Andhaa Kanoon*
Producer: A. Purnachandra Rao

Director: T. Rama Rao
Co-stars: Amitabh Bachchan, Rajnikant, Reena Roy

(1983) *Babu*
Producer: V.R. Parameshwaram
Director: A.V. Tirlogachander
Co-stars: Rajesh Khanna, Rati Agnihotri, Mala Sinha

(1983) *Ek Naya Itihaas*
Producer: B.S. Narayan
Director: Asha Devi
Co-star: Vinod Mehra

(1983) *Nastik*
Producer: Vinod Doshi
Director: Pramod Chakraborty
Co-star: Amitabh Bachchan

(1983) *Razia Sultan*
Producer: A.K. Mishra
Director: Kamaal Amrohi
Co-stars: Dharmendra, Parveen Babi

(1983) *Taqdeer*
Producer: Brij; Director: Brij
Co-stars: Shatrughan Sinha,
Mithun Chakraborty, Zeenat Aman

(1984) *Durga*
Producer: S.K. Kapur
Director: Shibu Mitra
Co-star: Raj Babbar

(1984) *Ek Nayi Paheli*
Producer: Subba Rao
Director: K. Balachander
Co-stars: Kamal Haasan, Raaj Kumar, Padmini Kolhapure

(1984) *Hum Dono*
Producer: Tony Glaad
Director: B.S. Glaad
Co-stars: Rajesh Khanna, Reena Roy

(1984) *Phaansi Ke Baad*
Producer: Harmesh Malhotra
Director: Harmesh Malhotra
Co-star: Shatrughan Sinha

(1984) *Qaidi*
Producer: G. Hanumantha Rao
Director: S.S. Ravichandra
Co-stars: Shatrughan Sinha, Jeetendra

(1984) *Raj Tilak*
Producer: Anil Suri; Director: Rajkumar Kohli
Co-stars: Sunil Dutt, Raaj Kumar, Dharmendra,
Reena Roy, Yogeeta Bali, Sarika

(1984) *Ram Tera Desh*
Producer: Tito
Director: Swaroop Kumar
Co-star: Shabana Azmi

(1984) *Sharara*
Producer: R.J. Chakravarti; Director: S.V. Rajendra Singh
Co-stars: Raaj Kumar, Shatrughan Sinha,
Mithun Chakraborty, Tina Munim

(1984) *Mrigtrishna*
Producer: Naheta Films
Director: Rajendra Shukla
Co-star: Yogeeta Bali

(1985) *Aandhi Toofan*
Producer: Pahlaj Nihalani; Director: B. Subhash
Co-stars: Shatrughan Sinha,
Mithun Chakraborty, Meenakshi Sheshadri

(1985) *Ramkali*
Producer: Ashok
Director: Shyam Ralhan
Co-stars: Shatrughan Sinha, Suresh Oberoi

(1985) *Yudh*
Producer: Gulshan Rai; Director: Ravi Rai
Co-stars: Anil Kapoor, Tina Munim,
Shatrughan Sinha, Jackie Shroff

(1986) *Anjaam*
Producer: Ramesh Tiwari
Director: Hariharan
Co-star: Shashi Kapoor

(1986) *Ek Chadar Maili Si*
Producer: G.M. Singh, Nindrajog

Director: Sukhwant Dhadda
Co-stars: Rishi Kapoor, Poonam Dhillon

(1987) *Apne Apne*
Producer: Ramesh Behl
Director: Ramesh Behl
Co-stars: Jeetendra, Rekha

(1987) *Hirasat*
Producer: Sunil Sharma
Director: Surendra Mohan
Co-star: Mithun Chakraborty

(1987) *Jaan Hatheli Pe*
Producer: Sudesh Kumar
Director: R. Jhalani
Co-star: Dharmendra

(1987) *Kudrat Ka Kanoon*
Producer: K.C. Bokadia
Director: Suresh Bokadia
Co-stars: Jackie Shroff, Raadhika

(1987) *Seetapur Ki Geeta*
Producer: S.K. Kapur
Director: Shibu Mitra
Co-star: Shoma Anand

(1988) *Mohabbat Ke Dushman*
Producer: Prakash Mehra
Director: Prakash Mehra
Co-stars: Raaj Kumar, Sanjay Dutt, Farha

(1988) *Mulzim*
Producer: G. Hanumantha Rao; Director: K.S.R. Das
Co-stars: Jeetendra, Shatrughan Sinha,
Kimi Katkar, Amrita Singh

(1988) *Rihaee*
Producer: NFDC
Director: Aruna Raje
Co-stars: Vinod Khanna, Naseeruddin Shah

(1988) *Tohfa Mohabbat Ka*
Producer: Mukesh Kumar
Director: Ram S. Govind
Co-star: Govinda

(1988) *Vijay*
Producer: Yash Raj Films; Director: Yash Chopra
Co-stars: Rajesh Khanna, Rishi Kapoor,
Anil Kapoor, Meenakshi Sheshadri, Sonam

(1989) *Desh Ke Dushman*
Producer: Manmohan Kapoor
Director: Swaroop Kumar
Co-star: Raaj Kumar

(1989) *Deshwasi*
Producer: Rajiv Goswami
Director: Rajiv Goswami
Co-stars: Poonam Dhillon, Manoj Kumar

(1989) *Paap Ka Ant*
Producer: Gautam Bokadia
Director: Vijay Reddy
Co-stars: Rajesh Khanna, Govinda, Madhuri Dixit

(1989) *Sachche Ka Bol Bala*
Producer: Dev Anand /Navketan Films
Director: Dev Anand
Co-stars: Dev Anand, Jackie Shroff, Meenakshi Sheshadri

(1989) *Santosh*
Director: Manoj Kumar
Producer: Balbir Kumar
Co-star: Manoj Kumar

(1990) *Jamaai Raja*
Producer: T. Trivikarma Rao
Director: A.K. Reddy
Co-stars: Anil Kapoor, Madhuri Dixit

(1990) *Lekin*
Producer: Hridayanath Mangeshkar
Director: Gulzar
Co-stars: Vinod Khanna, Dimple Kapadia

(1990) *Shadayantra*
Producer: Shakeel Khan
Director: Rajan Johri
Co-stars: Raj Babbar, Pankaj Kapoor

(1991) *Dil Aashna Hai*
Producer: Hema Malini; Director: Hema Malini

Co-stars: Shah Rukh Khan, Divya Bharati, Dimple Kapadia, Sonu Walia, Amrita Singh

(1991) *Hai Meri Jaan*
Producer: Roopesh Kumar
Director: Roopesh Kumar
Co-stars: Kumar Gaurav, Sunil Dutt

(1991) *Indira*
Producer: Balram Mohla
Director: Nripen Mohla
Co-stars: Suresh Oberoi

(1995) *Param Vir Chakra*
Producer: Ashok Kaul
Director: Ashok Kaul
Co-star: Navin Nischol

(1996) *Maahir*
Producer: Haresh Barot
Director: Lawrence D'Souza
Co-star: Govinda

(1996) *Swami Vivekananda*
Producer: Subi R. Reddy
Director: G.V. Iyer
Co-star: Mithun Chakraborty

(1997) *Himalayputra*
Producer: Vinod Khanna
Director: Pankaj Parashar
Co-stars: Vinod Khanna, Akshaye Khanna

(2000) *Hey! Ram*
Producer: Raajkamal Film International
Director: Kamal Haasan
Co-stars: Kamal Haasan, Rani Mukherjee, Girish Karnad, Naseeruddin Shah, Shah Rukh Khan

(2001) *Censor*
Producer: Navketan Films International
Director: Dev Anand
Co-stars: Shatrughan Sinha, Randhir Kapoor

(2003) *Baghbaan*
Producer: B.R. Films
Director: Ravi Chopra

Co-star: Amitabh Bachchan

(2004) *Veer Zaara*
Producer: Yash Raj Films; Director: Yash Chopra
Co-stars: Shah Rukh Khan, Rani Mukherjee, Preity Zinta, Amitabh Bachchan

II. FORTHCOMING

Baabul
Producer: B.R. Films; Director: Ravi Chopra
Co-stars: Amitabh Bachchan, Rani Mukherjee, Salman Khan, John Abraham, Sarika

III. GUEST APPEARANCES

(1972) *Garam Masala*
Producer: C. Mohan
Director: Aspi Irani
Co-stars: Mehmood, Aruna Irani

(1974) *Kunwara Baap*
Producer: Amarlal P. Chhabria
Director: Mehmood
Co-stars: Dharmendra, Amitabh Bachchan, Vinod Mehra, Mehmood

(1975) *Kehte Hain Mujko Raja*
Producer: Biswajeet
Director: Biswajeet
Co-stars: Biswajeet, Rekha

(1976) *Ginny Aur Johnny*
Producer: Amarlal P. Chhabria
Director: Mehmood
Co-star: Mehmood

(1976) *Barood*
Producer: Jugnu Enterprises
Director: Pramod Chakraborty
Co-stars: Rishi Kapoor, Shoma Anand

(1977) *Swami*
Producer: Jaya Chakravarti; Director: Basu Chatterji
Co-star: Dharmendra

(1977) *Chala Murari Hero Banne*

Producer: Advent Movies
Director: Asrani
Co-star: Asrani

(1977) *Shirdi Ke Saibaba*
Producer: Sarla Charitable Trust
Director: Manoj Kumar
Co-star: Manoj Kumar

(1978) *Cinema Cinema*
Producer: Shahab Ahmed
Director: Krishna Shah
Co-stars: Dharmendra, Amitabh Bachchan, Zeenat Aman

(1979) *Janta Havaldar*
Producer: Manoharlal P. Chhabria, Manohar P. Jaisingh
Director: Mehmood
Co-stars: Rajesh Khanna, Yogeeta Bali

(1982) *Suraag*
Producer: Jagmohan Mundhra; Director: Jagmohan Mundhra
Co-stars: Sanjeev Kumar, Shabana Azmi

(1996) *Jai Dakshineshwar Kali Maa*
Producer: Anuradha Paudwal
Director: Shantilal Soni
Co-star: Mrinal Kulkarni

IV. FILMS SHELVED

Galiyon Ka Badshah (no theatrical release, only on VHS)
Producer: Sher Jung Singh
Director: K. Yogee
Co-star: Raaj Kumar

Devdas
Producer: Kailas Chopra
Director: Gulzar
Co-stars: Dharmendra, Dina Pathak

Chanakya Chandragupta
Producer: B.R. Films; Director: B.R. Chopra
Co-star: Dilip Kumar

Aman Ke Farishtey
Producer: Kadar Kashmiri

Director: Dev Anand
Co-star: Dev Anand

Maarg

Producer: H.M. Creations
Director: Mahesh Bhatt
Co-star: Vinod Khanna

V. SONGS SUNG BY HEMA MALINI

'*Devdas mitua gaon…* '
with Kishore Kumar in *Haath Ki Safai* / 1974
'*Mujhe mat dua de ke main badduaa hoon…* '
with Kishore Kumar in *Dream Girl* / 1977
'*Meri galli mardon ka…* ' in *Indira* /1991

VI. TELESERIALS:

(1982) *Terah Panne*
Producer: Kiran Shantaram
Director: Vikas Desai
(1985) *Noopur*
Producer: H.M. Video Productions
Director: Hema Malini
(1991) *Adalat*
Producer: Dheeraj Kumar
Director: Dheeraj Kumar
(1994) *Mohini*
Producer: Zee Telefilms
Director: Hema Malini
(1994) *Naam Gum Jayega /Ahankar*
Producer: NFDC
Director: Sudipto Chattopadhya
(1995) *Rangoli*
Producer: NFDC
Director: Ramesh Talwar
(1996) *Yug*
Producer: Sattee Shourie
Director: Sunil Agnihotri
(1996) *Women of India*

Producer: H.M. Video Productions
Director: Lekh Tandon

(1997) *Aap Ki Saheli*
Producer: H.M. Video Productions
Director: Dinesh Chouhan

(1999) *Jai Mata Ki*
Producer: Cinevista
Director: Punit Issar

(2002) *Kamini Damini*
Producer: B.R. Films
Director: Ravi Chopra

VII. DANCE BALLETS:

Besides her innumerable solo Bharatanatyam dance performances all over the world, Hema has performed nine ballets (listed below) and two assorted dance shows *Nritya Mallika* and *Parampara.*

Meera

Producer: Natyavihar Kala Kendra
Choreographer: Bhushan Lakhandri
Writer: Maya Govind
Music: Shelly Dutta
Singers: Kavita Krishnamurthy, Ashit Desai
Stage/Lights: Paresh Daru/ Jayant Sahastabuddhe

Ramayan

Producer: Hema Malini For Indo-American Enterprises Inc., Los Angeles
Choreographer: Bhushan Lakhandri
Writer: Adapted from Tulsidas' *Ramcharitmanas*
Music: Ravindra Jain
Singers: Ravindra Jain, Suresh Wadkar, Kavita Krishnamurthy
Stage/Light: Gautam Joshi/ Jayant Sahastabuddhe
Sound: Markand Mehta

Durga

Producer: Natyavihar Kala Kendra
Choreographer: Bhushan Lakhandri
Music: Ravindra Jain
Singers: Ravindra Jain, Yesudas, Suresh Wadkar, Kavita

Krishnamurthy, Hemlata, Sushil Kumar, Aparna Mayekar
Stage/Lights: Tapas Sen, Jayant Sahastabuddhe, Chetan Merchant
Sound: Markand Mehta

Savitri

Producer: Natyavihar Kala Kendra
Choreographer: Bhushan Lakhandri
Music: Ravindra Jain
Singers: Ravindra Jain, Suresh Wadkar, Kavita Krishnamurthy, Hemlata
Stage/Lights: M S Sathyu /Tapas Sen
Sound: Markand Mehta

Mahalaxmi

Producer: Natyavihar Kala Kendra
Choreographer: Bhushan Lakhandri
Music: Ravindra Jain
Singers: Ravindra Jain, Suresh Wadkar, Kavita Krishnamurthy, Hemlata
Stage/Lights: Tapas Sen
Sound: Markand Mehta

Radha Krishna

Producer: Natyavihar Kala Kendra
Choreographer: Bhushan Lakhandri
Music: Ravindra Jain
Singers: Suresh Wadkar, Roop Kumar Rathod, Sadhna Sargam, Kavita Krishnamurthy, Mahalaxmi Iyer
Stage/Lights: Sudhir Arts

Geet Govind

Producer: Natyavihar Kala Kendra
Choreographer: Deepak Mazumdar
Music: Ashit Desai
Stage/Lights: Sudhir Arts, Shirish Mohan
Sound: Markand Mehta
Singers: Suresh Wadkar, Kavita Krishnamurthy. Mahalakshmi Iyer, Hema Desai, Sonali Vajpayee, Devaki Pandit, Ashit Desai

Draupadi

Producer: Natyavihar Kala Kendra

Choreographer: Bhushan Lakhandri
Music: Ravindra Jain
Singers: Suresh Wadkar, Kavita Krishnamurthy, Roop Kumar Rathod, Sadhana Sargam
Stage/Lights: Umang Kumar, Daniel Karkee
Sound: Markand Mehta

Yashoda Krishna

Producer: Natyavihar Kala Kendra
Choreographer: Bhushan Lakhandri
Music: Ravindra Jain
Singers Ravindra Jain, Suresh Wadkar, Kavita Krishnamurthy, Hemlata
Sound: Markand Mehta